Going In A Different Direction
The Most Epic Resignation of All Time
Youth Friendly Edition

Published By

Ray D. Martin Books

TM

Going In A Different Direction

The Most Epic Resignation of All Time™

ISBN 978-1975685638

Copyright 2018 © by Ray D. Martin Books

All rights reserved. Except for use in any review, the utilization or reproduction of this work in whole or in part in any form by any electronic, mechanical or other means, now known or hereinafter invented, including xerography, photocopying and recording, or in any information storage or retrieval system, is forbidden without written permission of Ray D. Martin Books. Submit requests to:

Ray D. Martin Books
18865 State Road 54
#327
Lutz, FL 33558

Although inspired by true events, this is a work of fiction. Names, characters, places, companies, and incidents are either the product of the author's imagination or are used fictitiously and any resemblance to actual persons, living or dead, business establishments, corporate entities, partnerships, events or locales is entirely coincidental.

For questions and comments about this work or to be notified of our next release, please contact us at raydmartinbooks@gmail.com. We would love to hear from you.

For My Readers

Thank you for purchasing this work. I am a passionate author that appreciates each and every reader and am confident you will enjoy the journey. This work is inspired by true events, however, great care was exercised to preserve the privacy of the characters and companies involved.

Ray

To Howard-

Proven leader, mentor, friend, proud father and Military Veteran. You were right, it's all about the people. Thank you for everything.

Going In A Different Direction
The Most Epic Resignation of All Time

CONTENT

CONTENT	vi
CHAPTER 1	1
CHAPTER 2	4
CHAPTER 3	15
CHAPTER 4	30
CHAPTER 5	42
CHAPTER 6	46
CHAPTER 7	55
CHAPTER 8	62
CHAPTER 9	65
CHAPTER 10	74
CHAPTER 11	82
CHAPTER 12	86
CHAPTER 13	89
CHAPTER 14	99
CHAPTER 15	105
CHAPTER 16	108
Epilogue	112

CHAPTER 1

Drenched in sweat, I stomped through the living room and into the kitchen to hand Kaitlyn her large vegetarian burrito and chips with salsa. I needed a shower.

"You're not eating?" she asked.

"I ate in the car," I yelled down the hall, stripping as I walked, while she followed me into the bathroom.

"You missed Aiden's game, today."

"I know," I responded, standing completely still under the showerhead and watching the water roll down the drain. "I only just remembered he had a game on the way home. It completely slipped my mind." I stood there wasting water for a few minutes, before I stepped out of the shower to face the music.

"He made another hat trick—his fourth of the season."

I had missed all four of them.

"Is it really necessary for you to go to the gym twice a day? I bet a healthy dose of youth lacrosse could ease just as much stress as a few pull-ups."

Kaitlyn was calm, but I had disappointed her and the kiddo, again. The fact that it was unintentional didn't lessen the disappointment. While I dressed, I ruminated on how I seemed stuck in a pattern—make a promise, forget said promise, break the promise, and deal with the aftermath of feeling like a disengaged father. It was a far cry from the days I coached his team, days I longed to see again.

"I'll be at the next one," I mumbled. "Is he mad? And where's Mitch? He didn't meet me at the door. My boy Boudreaux did, though," I said as I clapped, and my dog ran towards me—his big, brown eyes beaming—with his soggy tennis ball in his mouth, ready for a game of fetch.

"He's more sad than mad, and Mitch is at Nana's. By the way, we already ate. When I picked up Aiden after work, we went out. I left you a voicemail. I also sent you a text." Kaitlyn set a new bottle of my favorite aftershave on the bathroom sink. "I'm gonna go for a run, babe. I'll be back in about an hour. Nana will drop Mitch off here in about 20 minutes," she said, leaving the room.

I lightly rolled the slobbery tennis ball on the floor for Boudreaux again and again, as I thought of my former boss, Howard. Since the company let Howard go, I often wondered how he was doing. It didn't make any sense. Howard wasn't just the most decorated salesman at M Fisher Financial; he was the most personable, effective leader to ever come through. Other firms constantly courted him, but his supreme loyalty kept him at Fisher, even though a change could mean moving into the next tax bracket. Howard wasn't about the money; he was all about the people. So when he was backed into a corner and forced into early retirement, the entire sales staff was appalled. He did all the things he was supposed to do, and he got screwed for it. If Howard could be scrapped like fish bones, then what might they do to me, or to Jackson, or Cindy?

I snapped out of my thoughts. There was Aiden, standing in the door of our room, staring at me the way my father used to after receiving a phone call from my high school principal.

"You wanna tell me where you were today, Pop?" Aiden asked. "Because you said you'd be there, and you weren't."

"I know, son. I know. It slipped my mind. After work, I headed to the—"

"Gym. Yep," he said, interrupting to offer me a lacrosse ball. "Here's the game ball. They gave it to me—again. And you missed it—again." Aiden tossed the ball to me and walked away.

Not only had my work and health taken major blows, but the stress had found its way into my home. My breaking point was near.

CHAPTER 2

"So, I'm glad you're here," Hillary said, unconvincingly. She seemed annoyed, ready to scold. Hillary was Howard's replacement, an unworthy outsider from a different industry who didn't quite understand how things worked in finance. Ben, who had assumed the sales manager position below Hillary, was equally unworthy of his title. They hadn't been there long at all, but they made the office a little more toxic each time they swiped their access badges and entered the building. Never before had I wished to be sick, but unfortunately, I was well enough to go to work every single day.

Each January, our firm held its annual kickoff meeting to recap the fiscal year and inundate us with "I can" statements and positive metrics. I'm not usually one for a pep rally, but these meetings had been a highlight for me. Normally, cheesy music blared from the speakers, and macaroons and lattes from the corner bakery waited for us as we entered the conference room. Our eyes took in an embarrassing slideshow of group outings, the previous year's retreat, and the Christmas party, complete with the names of the previous year's top and most-improved producers. This year, as we walked into the ordinary meeting room, we were greeted by bottles of water and chairs arranged in rigid straight lines.

"When I took this position a few months ago, I was told that I was walking into a place of self-starters, real go-getters. But I'm looking at these numbers, and they say exactly the opposite," Hillary began.

Cindy and Sean caught each other in a glimpse, Cindy with furrowed brows, Sean with shrugged shoulders. Similar looks spread through the room.

"So, okay, take Cindy for example."

Cindy cocked her head to the side. Her face began to turn red.

Cindy made it a point to only say positive things about anyone. The closest I had ever seen her to discontent was the day she suggested we add tea to the drink selection in the break room. "I don't want to seem ungrateful, guys, but coffee kind of irritates my stomach. Could we add a few lighter options?" An assortment of tea was in the break room the next morning.

On her desk sat a picture of a cross in a frame, with the italicized text, "Speak only if what you have to say is more beautiful than silence." Considering all she had been through before she moved to town, including the back-to-back losses of her father and sister, it was amazing that her heart was still so tender. She became a little sister to Sean and me, so when we sensed that Hillary was about to strike, we sat at attention.

"I mean, Cindy, how do you explain a $37,425 drop in production from this time last year? How is that even possible? Seriously, explain it," Hillary sneered.

Cindy started, "Well, um," her voice began to crack, "the economy isn't in the best place right now, and I was in the hospital for a couple of months."

We were all aware of that. Hillary would have been, too, had she bothered to get to know any of us past our production spreadsheets.

"How long have you been back at work since the hospital stay?" Hillary asked.

"About five months," Cindy replied, reluctantly.

"That's plenty of time to get those numbers on the upswing, don't you think?" Hillary asked with scorn boldly written on her face.

Cindy stared at Hillary with her mouth open, unable to respond. For a while, we weren't sure she would even make it out of the hospital, and even though she had come back to work, Howard had given her all the leeway she needed to get back to 100%. He never said a word about her performance, especially since she was consistently one of our office's top ten producers.

Hillary began picking us off, one by one. She embarrassed us by sharing our drops in production, no matter how drastic, and met any upswings in production with, "It's good, but not great." By the time that meeting was over, Cindy was wiping the runny mascara from her eyes, and everyone else was livid.

I waited for the crowd to leave the room as Hillary sat at a table, marking something I couldn't make out on an employee file.

"Do you have a minute?" I inquired.

"Sure. Ray, right?" Wide, green eyes beamed through her oversized glasses. Hillary had called on me more than once in meetings, but suddenly, she wasn't sure of my name?

"Right," I answered, choosing not to dwell on it, as I pulled up a chair across from her.

"I was wondering if anyone briefed you on the culture of the office and the importance of the annual kickoff meeting. Did anyone happen to do that for you?" I clenched and released my fingers against the palm of my right hand, counting up to three and back down repeatedly, until I felt my jaws release.

"What about it?" she asked unyielding.

"This isn't exactly how the meeting is supposed to go. It's a time to lift employees up, to encourage them and lay out a plan to improve production in the coming months. It's certainly not a time to force people to air their laundry and berate them out in the open."

"Hmm ... Well, I wish someone would have briefed me on the fact that employees here are so sensitive and get their feelings hurt so easily. I mean, I thought that--what's her name-- Mindy?"

"Cindy."

"Yeah, Cindy. I thought that Cindy was going to need a paper bag to hyperventilate in, you know what I mean? This is her job, not an ice-cream social. Advising companies on their benefit offerings and financial strategies, especially folks of this caliber, is a hard job. Toughen up, or get out," Hillary said, as she continued writing on the folders. She was marking some of them in red with the word "EVALUATE" in all caps.

"That's a little cold, don't you think?" I asked.

"Excuse me, Ray? I know you've been here a long time, you're a top producer, yada yada, but you're out of line. I have a bachelor's in communications and a master's in public relations. I have more certifications than you'd probably care to count. I've done this for thirty years, and the awards on my wall at home prove that I'm well versed in how to handle employees in a company like this. I think I know what I'm doing. Have a good day."

I sighed, stood up, and left, absorbing my new reality.

❖

As the seasons began to change, so did my coworkers. The main hub of the office was looking a little sparser each day. Some colleagues were leaving by choice, others by force, without a trace. Of the people there, I now only recognized about half of them. The rest were new faces who only knew my name from plaques on the wall. They didn't make an effort to get to know me past that. Most of them were sure they'd learned all they needed to know from their high-priced business school classes. As a senior financial advisor, I could have taught them so much--and I wanted to--but they weren't interested.

Today was especially quiet. It was Saturday, and I should have been with my family, or tending to our charity. Instead, I was in my overly-decorated office. What used to be a place of excitement and potential now felt the way my bedroom used to when I was grounded as a teenager. My chest tightened as I lurched towards my desk to whittle away the stack of useless referrals. It hadn't taken long at all to secure the high profile clients I needed in order to remain the top advisor in the region. In fact, it took only five months to meet my goal for the year. I was on track to double that goal, until Hillary and Ben began to pass woeful prospects, that should have gone to newbies, my way. Researching investment options for my higher caliber clients, keeping them calm as the stock market volleyed, attending networking events, and following up with prospects who could bring millions to the company took time that I no longer had, thanks to these lame prospects Hillary and Ben tried to make me handle.

As I approached the bottom of the stack, I came across the final draft of my latest batch of business cards. Ms. Anita had signed off on them with her signature circle as the dot of the "I" in her name. The management we used to have knew that they had such a stellar team of advisors, any of us could walk away and make a go at a successful venture on our own. However, they provided a large platform, a wealth of resources, a home base, and a work environment that made us show up early just because, so we were happy to stay. The new management team didn't see things that way. They told us the week they came into power that we should consider it a privilege to work for a team with their level of experience and expertise. I tightened my jaw, but decided that I couldn't dwell on any of that now. I had convinced my friend, the recipient of a new patent, to meet with me that morning, so I could take a look at his portfolio.

I relaxed in my chair, squeezing a stress ball and looking out the window, waiting for Eric to arrive. I had known him from the gym and church, which is how I found out about the patent he was awarded for his purification system. He created this system with accumulated knowledge from working construction jobs on desalinization plants in the Caribbean. He invented a water purifier that he made from inexpensive parts and built in his garage, one by one. He had then donated them to mission groups in Haiti, several countries in Africa, and other regions that lacked clean water sources. Once he fine-tuned the design and received the patent, he sold the rights and earned millions. He knew I could help him plan for his future, so he came to see me.

Right on time, as was his way, he pulled into the visitor's parking spot, his camouflage F-450 with oversized tires and twin overhead exhausts taking up one-and-a-half-spaces. I don't think he ever really parked that way on purpose. I flipped through the notes I had made on him one last time before he arrived in the office, but when he hadn't shown up at my door five minutes later, I decided to go downstairs to check out what was taking him so long.

The elevator was out of service, so I took the stairs. I walked through the already-open door, and before rounding the corner to the lobby, I stopped to tie my shoe.

"You're here to see Ray, you said? He's pretty busy today, I'm sure, but I can help you," said Hillary. I had forgotten that she had planned to be there that day, running extra training sessions for the new recruits who were filling the places of the veterans who were leaving so quickly.

"Nah, we have an appointment," replied Eric.

"Well whatever he can do for you, I'm sure I can do right now. I'm not busy at the moment. Have you taken a look at our menu of services? A successful business owner like you wants to have his eggs in the right baskets. I can definitely show you the best options for your situation," Hillary pressed. "And while we're at it, we could take a look at your life insurance. We have a new whole life policy we just rolled out to our most preferred clients."

"Yeah, Ray mentioned it, but he said it's overpriced and has a poor credit rating. I don't think I'll waste my time with it. Thanks though," Eric replied. "Can you show me to his office? I'm on a schedule."

"Sure, but in case you have any questions after you meet with him, don't hesitate to come see me," she replied. I rounded the corner.

"Eric! What's up, man. What was the hold up?" I glanced in Hillary's direction as I waited for the answer.

"Just chatting with Hillary here, trying to get directions to your office. You ready?"

"Indeed I am. Follow me," I said.

"Who's she?" Eric asked on our way up the stairs.

"One of my new bosses, Hillary."

"She's pushy," he said.

"To say the least. What was she saying to you?" I asked.

"She just said that if I couldn't meet with you today, she could show me some portfolio options, something about you might be too busy. I told her we had an appointment, but I guess she didn't wanna hear that part."

"I guess not." We were in the office by now, and I had a bottle of water waiting for Eric on the desk by his seat. I offered him some bananas and a pack of almonds, which he gladly accepted. I remembered they were his favorite from a recent church picnic.

"You guys got any good vacation plans this year?" I began.

"The kids want Disney, Rhonda wants a beach, and I wanna hunt, so no," he laughed as he ruffled the imprint in his hair from his freshly removed baseball cap.

"A couple of friends of mine and I take a trip at the start of every deer season. You should join us this year," I said.

Eric was an avid hunter, so much so that he had a room in his house dedicated to his taxidermy collection. He talked about that collection for almost twenty minutes, and I listened, uninterrupted, taking mental notes about how his daughter was much more interested in hunting than his son, how she was an accurate shot, and how he wanted to retire early so he could knock off the list of places she would like to try her hand at big game, starting with Alaska.

"So how early are we talking for retirement? Ten years?"

"How aggressive does my portfolio need to be for me to do it in five? The guy at the other firm said we could do it in five" he answered.

"That's ambitious considering the size of the nest egg you said you wanted to accumulate. Not that I don't like ambitious, but part of my job is to give you realistic expectations. The market is just starting to come off its low, so assuming the economy cooperates, there is serious upside potential. However, there are many variables beyond our control affecting the markets. For example, geopolitical risk in Korea and the Middle East, interest rate uncertainty and the list goes on. We could be fine or it could be a real problem. Why don't we plan for seven years and hopefully achieve your goal in less time?

Eric slid back in his seat. "Seven is the best we can do?"

"Well that depends on two things. How well do you like to sleep at night, and how serious are you about your retirement timeline?"

"I enjoy sleep," he answered.

"Then let me propose several investment strategies with projected timelines. Let me do the worrying for you so you don't have to miss out on your family fun, and you can hopefully still retire sooner rather than later. Retirement's gonna be there, but those kids, you only got so much time with them." I took two of the profile folders off the table and opened the remaining one. I punched numbers into my fancy calculator, and laid both options in front of Eric.

"We could put 90% of your portfolio into a low-cost S&P 500 index fund, and likely turn your current account into over $10 million within thirty-six months. The remaining ten percent we should allocate into gold and bonds. This is an aggressive investment strategy, but with the market just coming off historic lows, the upside potential is huge and the fees are very small. We can always adjust your allocations at the drop of a hat as well. What do you think?"

"I like the plan. Let's go aggressive, and then I will check out whether we can do it in seven years, hopefully sooner. Sound good?" he asked.

"Sounds good to me, brother," I responded.

As I printed his final paperwork, we talked a little more about his annual camping trip, then shook hands before I walked him out. I was one step closer to earning another plaque for "Producer of the Year," however, it was much more rewarding to know that I gave him good advice.

CHAPTER 3

"I heard you stayed after that meeting the other day to talk to Hillary," said Jackson.

I rocked my office chair back and forth and popped a few M&Ms into my mouth while I stared out the window at the backside of downtown. I missed my simple workspace where we'd "prairie dog"—pop up, have a conversation, and then pop back down to the task at hand, each one of those talks threading us together a little more closely. Nowadays, the only thing that brought the sales team together was our names on the payroll.

"Yeah, but it wasn't that big a deal," I said.

"Well Hillary's been talking to people about it. I don't think she appreciated it very much," he said, raising his eyebrows and tilting his head to the side. "Not that I care. I told you about how she undercut me with the Stanford account, right?"

Jackson was the office hype man, and he had been at Fisher as long as I had.

"Yeah, you told me. That's so messed up. Why is she harping on our conversation? It wasn't even that big a deal," I reiterated.

Opening my mouth wide to finish off another pack of M&Ms, I felt a loud pop in my right jaw. That was the second time that had happened since Jackson came into my office. I grimaced and rubbed the side of my face.

"You alright, man?" Jackson asked.

"Yeah, I'm cool," I lied. My jaw was sore and tight, my teeth felt like they were each vying for position in my mouth, my shoulders were rigid, and I felt like I hadn't blinked in minutes. "I'll be fine."

Just then, Hillary banged my office door twice, then swung it open without waiting on an invitation to enter. She stood in the doorway.

"I need to see you this evening at five—my office," she barked before she turned on the heel of her stilettos and clicked down the hall without closing the door.

"Good luck, man," Jackson said as he exited behind her.

Sunshine poured through the walls of windows, reflecting off the white marble floors. Hillary's office, which sat vacant for a while before she was hired, now boasted two leather couches, one with reclining seats; a large stainless steel refrigerator; a bar, complete with a cappuccino machine; and a new chandelier. Without asking, I scooped a few of her fun-size candy bars into my hand for later.

"Nice office," I commented. Hillary sat at the head of the table, and surprisingly, didn't seem to care that I'd taken her snacks. Three sales managers surrounded the glass, wall-length conference table. I sat between two of them, feeling like the unsuspecting recipient of an addiction intervention. I hadn't seen these folks in months, since nowadays, their office doors were usually closed.

"Seems like you have a lot to say, Ray," Elliot said to open the meeting. Howard had hired Elliot before I started at Fisher, and the word was he was one of the main advocates for getting rid of Howard, but I couldn't be sure. "Would you mind telling us what's going on?"

"If you're talking about my staying after the meeting to talk about how it went with Hillary, I didn't think it was anything big. But while we're here, I don't mind letting everyone know that the kickoff meeting was an absolutely unnecessary public beat down of the staff," I said.

"What was so bad about it?" he asked, seeming earnest enough.

"You've been in those meetings every year, Elliot. It's a shame you missed this one. It was unlike anything I've ever seen in this office," I said. "Have you ever seen the movie *Glengarry Glen Ross*? The part where the sales team leader rips them all apart?" I asked.

He smiled. "Of course, that move is a classic."

"Well, this was way worse than that." I paused. "Cindy—you know Cindy—Cindy left there crying. For whatever reason, Hillary thought it necessary to give her hell in front of everyone, to blab about her drop-off in production down to the dollar, and disregard the fact that she was in the hospital for a while. I mean, Cindy of all people! What's happening here? What happened to this place?"

The room was momentarily silent, until Ben and Hillary made eye contact. Coming off a job at a state-run utility, I wasn't even sure what Ben had done to deserve a spot at the table. He didn't know much about our industry, and even less about how to interact with people. However, he was really great at affirming every low-blowing comment of Hillary's and bringing her lunch each day.

"Listen, Ray, I didn't appreciate what you said to me in there. In fact, I haven't appreciated your attitude here for a while. You leave work early, and from what I hear, it's just to go to the gym. You come in late sometimes because you've been working out. I mean, if you want to be in a gym so much, maybe you should look into being a personal trainer or something. Honestly, I'm not real sure what it is you want, but if you're going to be here, you need to get in line and follow instructions," Hillary lectured. "It's not even like you're in great shape," she added as she rolled her eyes. She was right. My workouts were sanity maintenance, not fitness competition prep. I ate whatever I wanted, which my waistline could attest to. I was tall enough that the few bonus pounds didn't make that much of a difference in my appearance. Additionally, Kaitlyn made sure my wardrobe was full of quality tailored pieces. Because of her, I was always well put together.

Unfazed by her comment about my fitness level, I continued. "What do you know about lines? Because from what I've been seeing from you, I'm not sure you have any." Despite my growing anger, my voice remained steady. "So please, tell me about lines, Hillary. Where was the line when you told Jackson's biggest client that he wouldn't be representing them anymore, but Jackson didn't find that out until he went to take that guy out for lunch and discovered you and your golf buddies at his office canoodling with that client instead? Was that the line? Or is the line at the checkout carts from these online shopping sprees you keep taking on company time?"

"Okay, Ray," Ben interjected, "you're clearly frustrated with the changes we've made lately. Tell me, if you were in one of our positions, what would you be doing differently?"

"For starters, I would treat the people who work here like people and not production factories who get treated like numbers and scolded for missing unrealistic production targets that you report to finance. Then, I'd make sure I was an example of appropriate workplace behavior. If I saw someone having a hard week or month or quarter, I'd provide the training and the direction to help them get their numbers up. Howard used to do all those things, but none of it is happening now. There are a lot of titles at this table, but not a whole lot of leadership. Management here used to lead.

I guess that left with Howard. Titles and leadership are not the same thing."

"Somehow I knew this was about Howard's leaving. But Ray, I don't know why you're mad about that. I thought it was pretty clear to everyone by now that Howard retired," Ben insisted.

Howard had been around for as long as I could remember. He and Dad were college buddies, and even though life took them separate ways after college—Dad to seminary, Howard to Officer Candidate School—they never lost touch. After Howard spent six years in the Army, he joined M Fisher Financial, his family moved down the street, and he spent many Sunday afternoons puffing cigars in the garage with my dad, while they talked about their favorite sports teams and the next presidential election, no matter how many years away it was. Our relationship consisted mostly of us saying hello when I would pass him on my bicycle on my way to ride through the neighborhood—that is, until my parents called on him to help me shuffle through a tough time, my junior year of high school.

My English teacher, Ms. Pierce, the underwhelming, shoulder-padded, nail-spitting head of the department, ensured that I knew she believed at worst, I would end up in jail, and at best, collecting baskets at a supermarket. She had mistaken my constant looking at the floor when she talked and one word answers to her questions for a bad attitude. In reality, my lack of confidence made it hard for me to look anyone in the eye, especially her. I shuddered at the sight of her; she looked as brazen as her perfume smelled, with a permanent frown etched onto her stone face alongside premature crow's feet. Her head was trapped by the petrified tilt of her neck, frozen that way from years of turning her nose up at students.

Under her rule, English class was as boring as she, and I was failing miserably. My parents were uninterested in any excuse for why I wasn't the head of the class like I had been my sophomore year. They believed heartily in education, so they did all they could to make sure I excelled, but my skipping class to hang out at the mall with my new friends wasn't helping the cause. My grades usually ebbed and flowed, but lately, they had been plummeting. Howard had gone through something similar with his own son, so when they saw the situation wasn't improving, despite parent/teacher conferences and the recurring loss of my weekend privileges, they asked Howard if he would hang out with me a few times a week.

"I'm not real sure what happened. It's like he went from super shy to super cocky, overnight. He's a good kid. Smart. We tell him all the time how glad we are to have him, and that he'll find his place eventually, but he doesn't hear it. Kids these days seem to listen to anybody but their parents, even if we're saying the exact same thing, so maybe he can hear it from you," I overheard Dad tell Howard in the garage. As much as I loved my parents, I was a bit relieved to get to spend time with Howard. My parents felt like they couldn't get through to me, no matter how hard they tried. Since Dad was a preacher, I was expected to be perfect. I wasn't perfect, and I'd grown tired of trying to be. Howard, who was always upbeat, seemed like the kind of guy I wished I could be like.

Our first meeting was out on the lake on Howard's boat, and that day, I realized why Dad spent his Sundays with Howard. I had never met an adult who was so easy to talk to. It seemed like he knew everything, but he wasn't a know-it-all. His awareness of the world was immense, and on top of that, he had features in his car that I'd never seen before. I couldn't wait to meet with him again. I needed to find out more about what he did for work.

Not long after we started meeting on the weekends, Howard's mother suddenly became sick. She died within a week of falling ill. We attended the funeral, and afterwards, Howard walked up beside me.

"I'm sorry for your loss, Mr. Howard," I said.

"Thanks, Ray." He looked straight ahead for a while, and then turned to me. "I'm gonna need somebody to help me tie up the loose ends, here. Would you mind helping me do a little bit of work on the house for the next few weekends? I can pay you for it."

"Yes, sir, I'll be here," I replied.
The next Saturday, I showed up at his mom's house at 6 a.m., ready to work.

Some of the stuff I already knew how to do, like mow the yard and prime the walls for painting. But Howard taught me how to fix a hole in the wall with spackle, and the difference between using mulch or pine straw for landscaping. I learned something new and exciting every weekend. I am not sure if the information was truly exciting; maybe it was just exciting because it was new, but I never grew bored of our conversations. I looked forward to them, all week.

Unintentionally, my English grades started to trend upwards, but that didn't change the fact that the tediousness of high school made each day almost unbearable. Howard usually tried to give me tips on how to make the days go by faster, but whenever I could lure him off topic, we talked about finance and economics, and I watched his eyes beam as he gushed on about stocks, entrepreneurship, and international trade. He opened my mind to new worlds.

"What's really going on with you and school, Ray?" he asked me one day on the way to the home improvement store.

"I just don't…I don't really like it. Everybody's always watching me, calling me PK and stuff. It's annoying. And school's too easy. It's boring."

"I understand that. It's not easy being a preacher's kid. But I gotta tell you, the more time you slack off, the harder it's gonna be to catch up. High school will be over before you know it. Then what are you planning to do?" he asked.

"I'm not sure. Maybe I can do what you do," I replied, hoping he'd confirm that I had what it takes.

"Maybe, but you gotta have discipline to do what I do. You gotta know how to deal with people, even people you don't necessarily like. Have you ever thought about joining ROTC? If you can develop discipline anywhere, it's there."

"You mean those kids who march around the schoolyard like they're prepping for war? No thanks," I replied.

"Why not? What turns you off about it?" he asked.

"My friends make fun of those kids," I mumbled.

"Well, are you the kind of man who lets other folks make his decisions for him, or are you the kind of man who makes his own decisions?"

"I know how to make my own choices," I asserted.

"Well, if that's the case, if ROTC interests you at all, you ought to give it a shot," he responded.

When I met with the school counselor about the following semester's schedule, I asked her if it would be possible to join ROTC in the middle of the year. She approved, and the day I received my uniform was the day I found a new sense of pride in myself. It took almost no time at all for me to realize that I loved ROTC. The camaraderie and teamwork I found there was like nothing I had ever experienced. I only regretted that I hadn't joined, earlier.

The days started to fly by, and my grades were looking better and better. However, as the end of my high school days approached, I realized I hadn't done enough to pursue the future in college my parents wanted for me. Maybe it wasn't too late. In a last ditch effort to try to get into college, I visited each of my teachers, asked them to average my scores, and begged for extra credit. Some of them complied, but most of them laughed at the impossibility of bringing my grades up to par with college admissions status. Ms. Pierce scoffed and waved her hand towards the door, quickly dismissing my request to do extra projects in my English classes. Even though he knew my academics had been lacking, Howard sat with me at my family's kitchen table several nights a week to help me fill out application after application, essay after essay. Every other Saturday, for four weeks, he showed up in the driveway in his black BMW to take me to colleges that were close enough for a day trip, just to give me a taste of campus life. His car always smelled of new leather. The more dorms I saw, the more fresh-faced college girls, the more football stadiums and gift shops drowning in sweatshirts of school colors, the more remorseful I felt in my lack of achievement over the years. But we didn't give up.

My mother was pleased with my efforts, no matter how late in the game they may have come. My father, supportive, but always the realist, would pass by the table where Howard and I worked, shaking his head in silence. He knew my toiling was in vain, but he didn't crush my spirit. I could sense his disappointment, which made me work harder.

Week after week, the envelopes began to appear in the mail. Each letter began with sentiments of regret. I only read one or two of them past the first line. Tired of rejection, I set my sights on a place I was almost sure to find acceptance.

Ever since I was a young boy, I had taken great pride in my country. I had a strong desire to serve the American people and an insatiable sense of duty, so when I realized college wasn't a possibility for me, I was glad that I had joined the school's ROTC; it gave me a taste of what a career in the military would look like. In April of my senior year, when the first Gulf War was the talk of the country, I was seventeen years old. I knew that I was meant to be there. My parents understood and gave me permission to enlist in the US Army. The day I signed those papers was the end of my youth. I was proud, not only to serve my country, but in my newfound manhood and independence.

Basic Training taught me a lot about myself. I learned that I was much tougher than I realized, but many of the young men who seemed to be the toughest were only acting. Take Private First Class Smith, for example, the most feared young soldier in our 66-man platoon. Smith was in excellent shape, he was the size of a professional linebacker, and we all thought he could storm hell with a bucket of water, until one day, we were on the receiving end of another random dusting, one of those times we were relentlessly berated for everything and no reason at all. When our leader was tired of yelling, he made us perform a series of impossible exercises until enough soldiers dropped or he got bored. That fateful day, halfway through the exercises, Private Smith melted into a puddle over his boots, sobbed with his hands covering his face, and walked away, shaking his head and mumbling something we couldn't understand. We never saw him again.

After graduation, we were sent to another base for advanced training. While this training was intense, it was a vacation compared to where we had just been. There, we were treated more like soldiers. At Basic Training we weren't much more than heads on bodies. I still laugh when I think of how Drill Sergeant Snodgrass yelled, "Head, what IIIIIIIIIIISSSSSSSSSS your problem? Why did you not hit the center of that target? You make me so mad that I want to slap my own momma!" Soon after I graduated, I realized how good a leader he really was. I learned more from him than any other leader in the military, including hand-to-hand combat, which would later save my life.

Soon after graduation, they pulled us in six-by-six to meet with a recruiting sergeant. There was good news and bad news. Fortunately, the war in the Middle East was de-escalating quickly, so we wouldn't be deployed. Unfortunately, many of us would be out of a job, although we would be honorably discharged.

Each of us received different offers. Mine was to be transferred to the Reserves, where I would be part of a large military intelligence unit. My GI Bill would be fully honored, I would go to college, and I would later be activated, if needed. They never gave me the alternative choice, and I only had a few minutes to make the decision, but to me, the other choice didn't really matter because this one was a pretty good setup. When the time allotted for me to come to a decision was up, I took the deal. I would be back home in time for Christmas.

And so, as my military days drew to an end, it was time to pursue the initial dream, again. Since I had taken some college courses through an outreach program while I served the country, and I had taken the SAT, I knew my chances of being accepted looked better than they had, before. This time around, the envelopes seemed to hold a different energy as I pulled them from the mailbox. The day I opened the letter that declared my acceptance into Howard's alma mater, I gained a new appreciation for that experience in the military and all the time Howard had spent helping me pull myself out of the muck. He was the first to learn of my acceptance.

Silently defending Howard's honor, I stared at Ben, each of us daring the other to blink first.

"Let me ask you, Ben, what is our company's most valuable asset? What's number one here? If we had to break the whole operation down into fragments and post one on the wall as the most important, what would that asset be?"

"Well, Ray, I'd have to say two things. First, the thoroughness and precision of our marketing research that leads us to a stream of new clients, and then, our size," Ben answered. I wondered if he realized his voice had changed and his posture had become erect, as if he were filming one of those local commercials that you hoped wouldn't air when your friends from out of town came to visit. His response was something from an unoriginal script. Part of me waited for the generic sound bite and jingle to play in the background. My stomach began to churn.

"Well, Ben, the number one asset used to be the people, so thanks for clearing that up for me. Are we done, here?" I asked, as I began to peel the paper off one of the candy bars I had grabbed from Hillary's desk.

"No, Ray, we're not done," Hillary interjected. "I'd appreciate a little more of your respect. You might feel a certain way about my qualifications to manage this office, but my accolades tell another story. You don't have to like me, but you will respect me. Get it in your head who's in control, here. If you don't need anything else, you can go," she said.

We stared at each other for several seconds before I stood to leave. "See you tomorrow," I nodded and forced a slight smile. It would take some time to prepare, but I knew I needed to start pondering an exit strategy.

CHAPTER 4

Initial meetings with potential clients were my specialty. Growing up, I was a chunky kid with thick glasses and a lisp, a combination that guaranteed relentless bullying from my classmates. My parents would have changed the order of the solar system for me, but they were the only ones who felt that way. Whenever I spoke, my classmates would begin to hiss. I spent many solo lunches at the corner table, thinking of ways to get the bullies to leave me alone. Nothing worked. They would constantly walk by and bump the back of my head with their backpacks, or stick their dirty fingers in the sandwich or soup thermos of my packed lunch. I knew what it was like to feel disposable. I never wanted to pass that feeling on to anyone else.

Even before my dad became a pastor, he would always seek out ways to help people in need. He would take meals to homeless people on the undesirable parts of town. He wouldn't just drop the food off, but he would sit and talk with them, for hours. He would anonymously drop off Christmas gifts to needy kids, if he knew their families wouldn't otherwise have a Christmas. One time, a kid in our congregation lost his dad in a car accident. My dad got me out of bed that night and took me over to the kid's house, so we could be there for the family.

"When we get there, don't worry about saying or doing the right thing. Just see if he needs anything, like water or another blanket or whatever, then sit next to him quietly, and listen. Showing up and listening are the best things you can do for somebody at a time like this. If you need me, I'll be wherever the grown-ups are." He told me that night, on our way to the bereaved family's home.

Those experiences developed empathy within me and it grew throughout my life. I tried to epitomize my father in my own leadership style in my business life, so I made it a point to make my clients and colleagues feel like superstars.

Taking a deep breath, I reached across my desk to call my clients who had birthdays that month to wish them well, but I paused when I heard Hillary and Ben walking through the office hallway, chomping a freshly popped bag of kettle corn that perfumed the hallway, snickering like a couple of hyenas.

"No regard for other people," I murmured and sighed. Part of me wished I would have shut my door completely instead of halfway, but I decided to stay put so they wouldn't know I was there. My intention was to ignore them, at first, until I heard Ben mention Jackson's name. If they were discussing my old friend, I felt obligated to find out why. I lowered the phone and listened intently.

"*Pathetic* is a good word," Hillary scoffed as Ben laughed.

"Yeah," he chimed in, "nobody will miss him, anyway. His book of business will be a good springboard for the newbies. I'm glad to see all the fresh blood in here."

"Me, too. He understands it was time for us to go in a different direction. Plus, those newbies are great at following orders. That's how it goes." Hillary was quick to add.

I pulled back from the phone, waited for the two jackals to clear the hall, then hustled to Jackson's office. It was empty. Suddenly, heat surged through my body, as I walked back to my office in disbelief.

In my early years, the office mantra was "People before profits," but since Hillary and Ben thought it necessary to cover up their thrice monthly verbal abuse sessions under the guise of developmental training, that mantra had become "Another day, another meeting." One particular day, leadership and several of the company's top salespeople got together for one of Ben's gatherings.

He began, "If you walked around the office today, you might have noticed that some of the offices are no longer occupied. We've been running the numbers, and we—as leadership—had to make some decisions to … cut the fat."

He paused so others could join in his laughter. Hillary was chuckling, as were three or four other people I didn't really recognize, but the joke was lost on the majority of the salespeople in the room. Annoyed, I zoned out and started thinking of the last of the good days, before Hillary's darkness completely took over.

❖

High-fives flew around the room like mockingbirds. Jackson had just officially signed three large companies, each to three-year contracts. He had closed all three deals within a week, which was a record for the company. Jackson's quarterly goal was to reach the amount that he had just made in a week, and since I had peer coached him through that goal, I wanted to share in his moment of pride. However, one of my biggest clients had decided not to renew a contract that we had held for several years. The tension wouldn't let go of my chest, so instead of dampening the celebration, I slid out of the break room and into my office.

A few minutes later, Jackson popped into my office. We had started together at Fisher, so he had known me long enough to know that if I didn't stick around for a celebration, there was a problem.

"I lost the Davis Trust account," I lamented. "You know, I've taken care of them for years."

"Really? Did they say why?"

"Not really, they just said they didn't want to renew with me, and if they changed their minds, they will reach out to me," I answered.

"Are you more upset about the loss of the money or the loss of the relationship?" he asked.

I paused. "Definitely the relationship. I really enjoyed working with them. The old man is a total prankster who got his girlfriend pregnant in high school, dropped out, and got a construction job to support his family. A few years after that, he started a homebuilding supply shop that grew into a $200 million enterprise. He is 70 now, still married to his high school sweetheart. They donate millions to charity each year. One time, they were in town for a game, and my wife, Kaitlyn, was able to get his group tickets right behind the bench on the 50-yard line. The game was sold out, so how she was able to do that, I couldn't tell you. But he wrote me a handwritten note after that, thanking us for the memory we helped him make with his grandkids and how he trusted how I was handling his future. It just doesn't make any sense that they would drop me without a reason or the courtesy of a discussion. I can only guess that someone came in and cut their fees significantly."

"Well, fix it. Give them a reason to reconsider. Find a way to remind them of the relationship they have with you. Make sure they know that they may save a few bucks, but nobody will care for them the way you do. Just call the old man and ask him what happened, man-to-man. He owes you an explanation. Let me know when you succeed." Jackson tapped my shoulder on his way out. His confidence gave me confidence.

I was able to reach the family patriarch, Mr. Davis, on his mobile phone, even though I was supposed to contact him through his attorney, first. After greetings and inquiries about his family, we got to it.

"What can I do for you, Ray?"

"Mr. Davis, we've known each other for a long time. Can I be straight with you?" I asked.

"Son, you know that's how I prefer my conversations and my whiskey," he answered.

"For my own sanity, I need to know why you didn't renew your contract with me."

"You're right. I shoulda called and talked to you about that. The family feels that our financial advisors and attorney need to be in the same city so they can have face-to-face meetings. I'm old school; I like everybody in the same room. Does that make sense?"

"Yes sir, it makes total sense. I'm glad to know that it isn't something I'd done, and I didn't realize your legal team wasn't here, anymore."

"Oh no, they're still here. Someone from your company told our attorney that you were relocating to California at the end of the year. She assigned a team of four or five people to handle our account, and to be honest, I think they're green and only seem interested in cashing commission checks instead of doing right by our investments," he said. This was the first I'd heard of any of this.

"I'm sorry, Mr. Davis, but I haven't the slightest clue what you're talking about. My family hasn't even thought about going anywhere."

"Seriously? Because the lady we talked to was pretty adamant about it."

"Yes, seriously," I answered.

"In that case, give my attorney a call and set a meeting. If you're not going anywhere, neither am I."

And just like that, I had the account back, along with one of my closest client relationships. Without Jackson's insight, I might have just ruminated over it until I drove myself nuts. Once I found out about what had really happened, I knew something was up. I just wasn't sure yet what it was.

Jackson's commitment to the entire office's excellence didn't matter to Hillary and Ben. They fired him without notice and gave his hard-earned business to a selection of new hires they had just recruited from smaller companies. I couldn't help but wonder if the new leadership had promised the recruits Jackson's accounts in advance. They knew they would get rid of him and could spread out his $2 million in revenue among eight people. That way, if one of those people left, the hit to the division's revenue would not be nearly as bad. Had Jackson known he was on their hit list, he could have left on his own terms and taken his clients with him.

I focused back in on the meeting, which only grew more uncomfortable as Hillary and Ben continued calling out our sales numbers from the previous quarter, not for the sake of celebrating successes, but for the sole purpose of embarrassment.

"It looks like Rebecca decided to take a few months off," Ben said. "Her numbers are a freaking joke. If she doesn't get it together after this quarter, she might as well just go on over to the folks at the firm down the street and join their mediocre sales staff. She'll fit right in there—average."

I looked around the room, wondering if I was in some alternate universe—was anyone else hearing the same thing? Howard and my dad would be disappointed if I just sat back and let this happen.

"That's enough, Ben. These are our coworkers, our friends. You don't know Jackson like we do. You don't know Rebecca like we do. Those folks have given everything to this company," I said.

"Well, it's clearly not enough. We're setting goals here, and they're coming up short" he quipped as he looked around the room, fishing for approval from the recently hired sales managers who were doing a bang-up job of micromanaging us. "Maybe you should tell your friends to step their game up—well, Rebecca anyway. Jackson is done. We had to go in a different direction."

"Well, I, for one, don't appreciate you talking about them like that." I was far from ready to put up with his unflattering remarks.

Ben raised his eyebrows and shrugged his shoulders. "Okay, whatever. Back to what I was saying." I decided not to speak another word for the rest of the meeting.

Ben had come into the office on his first day and intentionally met each one of us, stopping to get our names and shake our hands. I was impressed that he still remembered our names that afternoon. Even though Hillary had hired him, he didn't seem anything like her. Ready to help the new guy feel like part of the family, and hoping to get a feel as to whether he would provide a buffer between us and Hillary, Jackson and I invited Ben out to lunch.

"It seems like this is a great place to work, man. Everybody has made me feel right at home," Ben said as he waited for his salad.

"Yeah, there are a lot of changes right now, but we're optimistic that the atmosphere will improve," I responded. "So tell me about your family."

"My wife and I have been married for 15 years. I had been with my last company for a long time, and we felt like it was time for a change. I had been trying to get into this industry for years. We should get together sometime. I saw the picture of your wife, sons, and dog on your desk. Lovely family," Ben said with a complimentary smile.

"Thanks, I appreciate that. So what's your management style? What's your philosophy?" I asked.

"My job is to steer the boat and keep the crew focused and alert so we can stay afloat, know what I mean? I do all I can to make that happen," Ben said.

"Then you should do just fine," I responded. We enjoyed our lunch, I paid the bill, and we headed back to the office. As time went on, Ben's ideas of how he should keep the boat afloat morphed from encouraging us with handwritten notes and weekly visits to each of our offices, to simple emails. From there, he began to make snarky remarks about us in front of other employees, scoffing if our numbers didn't meet his arbitrary standards, and it didn't take long to realize he was doing the same thing behind our backs. The crew was starting to jump ship, and Ben was struggling to steer the boat.

In just a matter of months, Ben started to lose control, and the morale of the office continued to decline. I knew I needed to protect myself. There was no telling what he was saying about me when I wasn't around.

After the meeting, he approached me and asked me to stay in the meeting room. He skipped all the formalities and got right to it.

"You've been here a while, Ray, and you've served us well."

I didn't respond.

" I saw your numbers from the last five years, and I must say, they're very impressive, especially considering that you are about ten years younger than most other senior producers in the office."

I was surprised that he even recognized my accomplishments at all. I could sense the "but" was coming, as he leaned in closer.

"Maybe you've done all you can do, here. You don't really have much further up to go. Have you ever considered leaving the industry altogether, and doing something totally different?"

To say I was befuddled would have been an understatement. I searched my brain for a response, but nothing would come to me.

He smiled and said, "Don't get me wrong. I'm not saying that you *should* leave the industry. I was just wondering if you had ever thought about it."

It took me no time to realize what he was trying to do, and just as quickly, I decided I was above it. Perhaps he read the nodding of my head as agreement, so he continued.

"For example, have you thought of running your charity full-time?" Of course, he knew that wasn't a financially sound possibility, even if I had been considering a career change.

"By the way, how is that dog of yours? Is old Cujo even still around?"

"His name is Boudreaux," I answered, looking at him straight in the eyes.

We glared at each other, and I considered whether the satisfaction of choking him would be worth the legal ramifications. He didn't stop there.

"I'm just saying, man, maybe you should think about it, you know, trying something else. Hey, you know what! Maybe you and Jackson could go do something together. You've got the know-how. I just wonder if you haven't outgrown this place."

"Thanks, Ben. Have a good day," I said, ending the conversation.

I walked down the hall toward the elevators, and fuming from the talk with Ben, I decided that no matter how long I stayed at Fisher, I wouldn't be attending any more of those meetings. It wasn't like they would miss me; this new management was so caught up in numbers, they barely even noticed faces. A stale, lifeless culture overtook the office for the next two years.

CHAPTER 5

Boudreaux held on far longer than Kaitlyn and I expected. He passed away on February 9, exactly ten years to the day that we moved into our new home. He knew it was home the second he arrived. He sprinted through the door and rolled around on the carpet for hours, making sure that everyone knew this was his domain. We splurged on floor-to-ceiling windows so that he could look outside from almost anywhere in the house.

My wife found Boudreaux in a swamp while on a bayou tour in Baton Rouge. The captain spotted the dog on the shore near an alligator. Boudreaux jumped into the water and swam toward the boat. A guide on the boat jumped in and plucked him from the swamp before the gator could notice him. The homeless dog followed my wife around the boat the whole tour, so the next day, she bought him a plane ticket. We guessed that he was around seventeen years old when he died. Boudreaux should have died that day in the swamp, but instead he found a loving family, and we gave him a full life. He was a great dog and companion. I still missed him very much and longed for the days when he rested his head on my shoulder, as I softly stroked his ear.

One day soon after, as I sat in my home office, squeezing one of Boudreaux's favorite squeaky toys, I received a phone call from an executive recruiter, a lady who sits on the expansion board with me for our children's school, who called me around the same time every year to see if I was ready to "make a change."

"Hey Ray, this is Suzy from JR Executive Search."

"Hey Suzy, how's it going?" I wasn't especially enthusiastic.

"I'm living the dream," she answered.

"Great. What can I do for you?"

"I need a favor. This is an odd request, but one of your leaders is a finalist for a high-ranking position at one of our client's firms. He has applied for many positions throughout the industry, which has us concerned. This may put you in an uncomfortable position, so if you'd rather not discuss this with me, I certainly understand."

"Okay, who do you need intel on?"

"Ben Bonaparte" she said.

"Really? As in Ben, one of my sales managers?" I asked, feeling slightly amused.

"Yes, that's him," she replied. I could tell she was a little apprehensive about what I might say next.

"Well, Suzy, our company has very strict policies when it comes to commenting on things like this."

"I know, and I feel bad putting you in this situation, given our history, but he is a finalist, and to be honest with you, he concerns me. The problem is, I don't have any evidence as to why. It's just my instinct," Suzy said.

"Really? What does your instinct tell you?"

"That he is a weak leader, a shameless self-promoter, and he can't be trusted." After what he'd said to me days prior, I had no qualms confirming this information with Suzy.

I had to laugh, but I couldn't confirm her suspicions outright. "Instead of giving you my opinion, how about I tell you honestly what it is like to be around him? This will allow you to make your own decision. It does break my company's policy, but these are true events, so what I say can't be considered slander."

"That would be great, Ray! I can't thank you enough."

"Well for starters, he doesn't mind bad-mouthing employees, behind their backs or in front of other people. He asks us to do extravagant tasks to try to get leads and clients while he plays on his cell phone most of the day. We had this weird conversation a while back, where he commended my hard work, and then suggested I leave and go do something else. And um," I debated for a few moments on whether to make the next petty statement.

"He never picks up the tab at lunch." She was relieved, and she thanked me over and over for confirming her instinct.

"Ray, this is going to disappoint the search committee immensely. I expect they will question its accuracy."

"Then have them call me. Give them my mobile number."

I never received a call from the search committee. However, the next week, I did receive a couple of hundred dollars in gift cards to my favorite fast-casual chicken restaurant with a note that said, "Lunch is on us." My kids' faces lit up every time we passed the yellow, red, and blue sign, and I understood; my heart skipped a beat when their grilled Thanksgiving turkey sandwich made its appearance, each fall.

CHAPTER 6

"Happy birthday, baby," Kaitlyn whispered in my ear to wake me. I hadn't even realized the date.

"Thanks, babe," I said, mustering up a smile. "Do you have anything planned?"

"I asked you a few days ago if you wanted to do anything. You just said you'd think about it and let me know."

"Yeah, I can't think of anything. I think I'll just go to the gym after work." I had overslept and missed my morning workout anyway. When I yawned, my jaw popped loudly and painfully. I rubbed the side of my face.

"You were grinding your teeth all night, Ray. You need to get that checked out, maybe get a mouth guard or something?" Kaitlyn said.

"I'll be fine."

I threw on my work slacks from the day before and a fresh shirt and started to prep my bag. Gone were the days when I wore suits to work. I just didn't care anymore.

"I know things are bad. What can I do?" Kaitlyn rubbed my arm, then ran her fingers over my stubbly head. I had woken up too late to shave it.

"I honestly don't know. I don't think there's anything you can do."

"Well, if you need me to swing by and, I dunno, key somebody's car, I'm there for you, babe." I knew she wasn't joking.

"I just hope this is over with sooner rather than later," I said.

"Me too, because I'm worried about you. Work is wearing you down, plus you're serving on the board at the school and doing work with the foundation. Your stress medication—I mean, I know it's supposed to help—but that stuff isn't good for you. I need you here, sweetheart. I don't wanna lose you to a heart attack."

"I'm gonna work this out, baby. I am," I tried to assure her.

Several years ago, the morning of one of my birthdays there at the firm, I walked into the elevator and smelled pancakes. I hadn't wanted to get too excited, but I hoped that what I thought was about to happen was about to happen.

To my surprise, I stepped off the elevator to a chorus of coworkers singing Stevie Wonder's version of "The Birthday Song," led by Miss Anita, who had more flavor than a bowl of jambalaya. When birthdays rolled around, she went out of her way to make them special for us. She organized the breakfast, ordered the cake, and decorated our cubicles before we arrived to work that day. No one could fly under the radar with Miss Anita around.

"Happy Birthday, Ray! I talked to Kaitlyn and made sure I got all your favorite things here, today," she seemed to sing as she hugged me so tightly, I could smell her perfume on my shirt for the rest of the day. She rocked from side to side, and when she loosened her embrace, she handed me an envelope with my name written in calligraphy on the front. I opened it and found a gift card to the coffee shop down the street. Miss Anita winked and ushered me towards the food.

Against the wall was a buffet of breakfast heaven: bacon; an omelet bar; an assortment of fruit, coffee, and juice; and of course, pancakes, complete with cooked-in blueberries and warm syrup.

On my desk was a bouquet of balloons with one that stood out above the rest. "Happy Birthday," was on one side; "Chump" was on the other. I laughed. My coworkers had filled my drawers with all my favorite candy, but the best gift of the day was the bobble-head doll that they had designed in my image, complete with black, square-rimmed glasses.

Howard came out of his office after a call with much pomp, and stood in the front of the room.

"What can I say about Ray?" he announced with one hand raised. Everyone chuckled.

"I've known him since he was a wee lad, weird, the way we all are in middle school. There were days when I wasn't even sure the kid could read, and now, look at him. They say he's been Advisor of the Year or something once or twice, I don't know." Jackson grabbed my shoulder. For three consecutive years, Howard had presented me with the company's "Epitome Award," which went to the person who demonstrated leadership, selflessness, and kindness throughout the office. The employees voted on it, and each year, I was humbled and choked up with pride to have received it. After Howard left, the new leaders replaced the "Epitome Award" with the "Engaged Award." It was basically for the employee who drank the most corporate Kool-Aid with the biggest smile.

"I could take credit for the young man's success, but I won't. No, seriously, Ray, we're all glad you're here. You're a wonderful example of what a father, husband, an advisor, and a friend should be. Happy Birthday, buddy." He looked at me and gave me a nod. Everyone raised their orange juice glasses for a toast before we devoured the breakfast buffet.

Today, there was only silence. Somebody was in the corner printing papers. One person was at her desk, playing a memory game on her phone. Half the lights were off. I missed the birthday celebrations of balloons and pancakes. I sat and turned on my computer to check emails. There was one from corporate with the subject line "Happy Birthday." I rolled my eyes as I clicked on it.

Happy Birthday, Pal.
Have a "hoppy" day.

There was a frog on there, or so I assume. The picture wouldn't open, so there was just a box with an x in the corner. It might have been a bunny. Considering who sent it, it could have been a snake. I deleted the email and prepped for my meeting with a new prospect.

"How are you?" Sean asked, his hands wrapped about his cup of black coffee. It was warm for the beginning of December, so we sat on the café's patio. I was always glad to be around Sean; he had a way of making me feel important. Surprisingly, he never married, which always made me scratch my head. Maybe he just enjoyed his freedom. I don't know; I never asked. He sent encouraging emails if he sensed a colleague was having a bad day, he secretly slid envelopes of money into people's desks if he learned of anyone's financial hardships, and he bought Christmas presents for unfortunate kids at local schools.

Sean was an exceptional guy, but our bond went beyond celebrating milestones at work and clowning around at office parties. We had the kind of connection you form with someone when you have been through tragedy, together.

Early in my career, Sean and I were attending an event at the office of one of our mutual clients. Since it was the middle of the week, we decided to leave early—around 8:00 pm. Earlier that evening, I had dropped my car off at a high rise to ride with him, so he dropped me back off there.

"Thanks for the ride," I said.

"Let me walk you to your car," Sean offered.

"No, I'm good," I responded.

"Come on man. You're tough, but you're not Super Man. Let me walk you to your car," he insisted.

"Why, so you can hold my hand? I'm good, man. I'll see you tomorrow. Thanks, again." I closed the passenger door of his SUV and headed up the staircase to my parking spot.

All I remember after that is struggling to keep a knife from my throat. I could feel the sting of cuts all over my body. Somehow, I got out of there and ended up in the street in the middle of downtown, where the police found me in a pool of blood and took me to the closest trauma center.

It took about a month to be able to walk without the use of a cane, and most of the nerve damage was expected to heal, but the mental ramifications of the event wouldn't depart so quickly. I was diagnosed with Post Traumatic Stress Disorder, and ended up having to take several medications that didn't work as well as my doctors had hoped. I didn't tell people about the PTSD, but it was a daily, hourly battle to stay in a workable headspace, especially since I couldn't determine triggers that flashed me back to that awful evening.

Sean felt responsible for a long time, until he was finally convinced that the event wasn't his fault. He offered to walk with me to my car, more than once. I declined. He did all he could to help me recover, which was good enough for me.

I sighed, then raised my eyebrows and started biting the inside of my right cheek. "I'm dying out there, man." Sean and I began working at the firm around the same time, and the entire time we worked together, he maintained his spot as one of the top five salespeople on the leaderboard.

"Be more specific, Ray. You look like hell, that's for sure. I mean, you have dropped some spare pounds, but your eyes …" Sean took a sip of his drink, "like hell."

I tapped my fingers on my cup. "It's nothing like it used to be here. We're not getting business through the network like we used to. We have all this management in the office, but they're not doing anything but watching our every move. They berate us in these meetings. They do underhanded stuff, like snatch quality clients from good advisors. Nobody's ever demanded to know who our prospects were, before, but they sure do, now. And what's up with the canned PDF birthday and anniversary emails? This place has gone to hell since Howard left. It's like watching a wrecking ball plow through your favorite arcade."

"I know. How's Kaitlyn doing with all this?" Sean added a packet of artificial sweetener to his drink. I started to lecture him about how unhealthy a choice that was, but I lacked the will. Plus, I hadn't been making the healthiest choices myself. I let it pass.

"I think exasperated is a good word, but you know Kaitlyn. She's amazing. I don't feel like I spend nearly as much time with my sons as I should. I didn't want to do anything but go to the gym—alone—for my birthday. When I'm home, I'm totally disconnected. She's amazingly supportive, so she won't nag or throw a fit, but she's got to be sick of this. I know she is," I gushed as I finally began to drink my coffee, also black. "How's business going for you?"

"It's good for me, personally, but I don't like the new atmosphere, you know? I feel like it's impossible to get as much done as we used to, and we can't build client relationships like we used to either."

"Right? The never-ending meetings, constant red tape, backstabbing, and no answers to any questions of substance. Plus they are pushing us to increase client fees, all the while reducing the support that they will give to our clients. Do more with significantly less."

"Yep," Sean agreed. "I wish things would change, but does it make sense to try to be a savior once all the good people who understand the culture of the company are gone? I could be naïve and pretend like I make a difference, but I see what's happening right before me. I had already been thinking of going out on my own, but now, I'm doing more than just thinking about it. What are you gonna do?"

"I'm not sure," I murmured.

"My suggestion?" He took a long sip. "Don't wait until you become someone you don't like. Life is too short."

Sean stood up, picked up his cup, and pushed in his chair. "I'm here if you need me," he said.

I sat at the table, relieved by Sean's confirmation of what I already knew. I wasn't blowing anything out of proportion. The company was becoming the corporate nightmare I had been lucky to avoid since I signed my contract years ago.

"So what are you going to do?" I asked Sean.

"Leave." He didn't hesitate.

"Wait—as in like, leave the company?"

"Exactly. This ship's been sinking since Howard left. I ain't hanging out for this train wreck."

"When?"

"At two o'clock today." And just like that, we had lost one more of the good ones. He would have stuck around if things were still all about the people. I was wondering more each day what I was still doing there, myself.

CHAPTER 7

I felt my teeth clench as I walked into Hillary's office, later that afternoon. Diffusers were all over the place, emanating essential oil smells that one would find in a yoga studio. On her conference table were three shopping bags. One of her tablets was open to a shopping site, which made me wonder—and not for the first time—how much time she actually spent working at work. I heard the click of her heels on the floor as she headed toward the office—late, like normal.

"What did I ask you to do? Because I'm pretty sure I asked you to return the magenta ones and the midnight ones, and order them in the smaller size, right? I mean, if you can't figure out how to do that much, I could hire a monkey off the street to do it. It's not like this is difficult. Figure it out," Hillary barked at her assistant before flouncing into the office where I stood, then slamming the door.

"I heard you closed the Richardson account, Ray. That was set aside for somebody else. We had been communicating with Debbie Richardson for months about handling her family's portfolio, and I was grooming several of the new advisors to take it over. That portfolio is worth $200,000 in annual revenue from servicing fees alone. Not to mention selling them our new whole life insurance policy, which has the industry's highest sales commission. Ben and I were the only ones who knew about it, so you plan on telling me how you even got wind of it?"

"Hello, Hillary. I'm fine today, glad you asked. And I can see you're… as usual. But yes, I closed the Richardson deal, and if I'm not mistaken, it might just be the biggest deal that this office has seen since Howard left, so you're welcome." I responded.

"How did you find out about it?" she pressed.

"Debbie Richardson called me directly months ago. Her grandchildren and my sons go to the same school. We also serve on the Board of Directors together. In fact, last year I smoked 60 pounds of barbeque to serve at her house for one of the school's fundraisers. Our families see each other often. She appreciates the work I do for the school and she trusts me. I wasn't aware that you and your buddies were competing with me for their business. Can't say I care either."

"Fair enough. When will we get paid?" she asked.

I stood there looking at her, bewildered. "When will we get paid," I managed to say as I swallowed a huge lump in my throat. "You know, most managers would congratulate an advisor for winning such a large account. Maybe she called me because I've been doing this for years and your new guys are a little too new. You should be glad that she decided to go with someone in our firm, even if it wasn't who you wanted it to be."

"You should be glad that I'm even signing the paperwork to let the commissions go through to you" she muttered before turning and strutting out the door. I walked out right behind her and headed to the human resources office.

❖

"I need to file a complaint against Hillary," I said confidently to the human resources director.

"Jump in line, my friend," she responded. "You're the third one, just this month."

"Are you kidding? How's she dodging the consequences?"

"It's all about who you know, Ray. We acquired her family's company," she said matter-of-factly. "Hillary is protected way up the chain. Nobody could touch her if they wanted to."

"What about Ben? How can a backstabber like that stay employed?"

"Simple," she answered. "He's her puppet. Puppets stay safe." she gave me a mischievous wink.

"Who else filed complaints, Scarlett?" my curiosity got hold of me.

Scarlett looked at me over the top of her glasses. "Now you know I can't tell you that." She started to whisper, "But I can tell you that one of them isn't here anymore." She slid back in her chair and popped another breath mint into her mouth.

"What's up with the breath mints, Scarlett?" I asked, chuckling.

"Yeah, well, they're less calories than chocolate, and I'm on a diet." Scarlett ate another breath mint. I laughed as I sat down to go through the process of filing a complaint about Hillary's daily tardiness, online shopping sprees on company billable time, and delivery of personal items to work, not to mention the incessant bullying, condescending behavior, and abusive language.

Later that week, Scarlett called me into her office. Thinking that maybe they needed more information about the complaint, I readily complied, but when I arrived, I learned that she had called on me for something altogether different.

My charity, which aided families of first responders, was suddenly under scrutiny. Most everyone at the office knew about the organization. They had attended events for the charity, and many of them had even made donations, which was why I was perplexed when Scarlett took an hour of my day to grill me about the organization.

"Hey Ray, I'm sorry to interrupt your day with this, but I just need to ask you some questions," Scarlett began. After asking questions about the basics, like when the organization was established and where, she began to get more specific.

"Who was involved in its creation?" she asked, clicking her pen incessantly.

"Just me and Kaitlyn. We put this thing together," I answered.

"So nobody else within the company?"

"No, this isn't a work thing. This is personal. I saw a need for it during my stint in the military and decided that once I was able, I would do something to help these families."

"Okay, so, if we looked at the terms of ownership, it would just say—"

"Me and Kaitlyn."

"Okay. What about the financials? How is that arranged?" still not looking up from her paper.

"Well, if you're asking where the money comes from, it's all donations and fundraising events. You know this, Scarlett. You've given us donations, before. If you need more specifics you can view our annual 501C3 financials on the internet. Could you tell me what this is really about?" I asked.

"We just—the company just—we just need some things cleared up," she replied.

"Who is we?" I asked.

"We just need to know some things," she answered.

I was in that room for only a few minutes before it was clear that Hillary was behind this. Certainly, she had gotten wind of my complaint and was making the effort to retaliate. At that moment, I decided that I couldn't control her actions or anyone else's, but I could control my responses. I answered every question with poise, ensuring that no one could use anything I said in the recorded conversation against me.

"Who runs your website?"

"A friend of mine has a son who handles websites. He does it for me," I answered.

"And does that friend work here at Fisher?"

"No, no he does not."

"We know that there is a software program that you helped develop for the charity, but we're not sure what it does. We don't really need to know that, per se, we just want to know if you used any resources from your job here to create or implement that software in any way," Scarlett said. She took a deep breath and scratched her forehead.

"I never worked on that software here. The most I've ever done in relation to the charity here is ask people if they wanted to contribute to the end of the year drive, and invite colleagues to the black tie fundraiser, that's it. Nothing else," I answered.

"Nothing else?"

"Nope," I told her. This is my charity. Nothing more, nothing less. For a moment, no one said anything else.

"Look, Scarlett, being a soldier, or a police officer, or a fire fighter, or in any careers where people's lives are in your hands—that's stressful enough on families. They don't ever know if their loved ones are coming home, and sometimes, they don't come home. When they don't, my non-profit just wants to make sure that these families don't have to worry about as heavy a financial burden as they'd have to worry about, if we weren't there. That's all," I tried to assure her.

"I understand, Ray. And I and everybody else in this office appreciate your work. Almost everybody else," she added.

Scarlett stood up and apologized for wasting my time. I smiled, shook her hand, and went to my office.

CHAPTER 8

That day, I met a friend and former client for lunch. He had gotten wind that many people in the company were unhappy and looking for other jobs, and he figured I would be at the top of that list. After we talked about football and a little bit about how his business was going, he tipped me off that a buddy of his, who worked for one of our main competitors, Triad Financial, was about to sign an employment contract with our firm—and he wasn't the only one. Multiple salespeople were leaving Triad to join Fisher. My eyes popped open, and I couldn't think of anything to say, nor could I understand why the heck they would want to jump onto what appeared to be a sinking ship. I later realized that they'd been promised hefty books of business that would be left over once a mass firing took place, and the word was they were enticed with small signing bonuses to move them in our direction. I figured if they were leaving Triad for Fisher, Triad must have been a despondent place to work.

Later in the week, during my commute, my phone began to buzz. When I saw Hillary's name flash on the screen, I took a deep breath. "Responses instead of reactions," I said to myself again and again before answering.

"Good morning, Hillary," I answered with a smile, hoping she could feel my manufactured positivity across the phone line.

"How's my…favorite producer doing, today?" She left no time to answer. "I just wanted you to know that we have made a decision that will affect your business," she said smugly. The call sounded strange. She had me on speakerphone, which let me know that Ben was probably in the room, and there's no telling who else.

"I know. I heard from a client. You hired some of the guys from Triad, right? I think that's brilliant. I've already started planning a welcome lunch for the entire department. I have a few opportunities to bring them in on that will get them some money right away and teach them how we do things. I like those guys." As soon as I finished talking, my jaw tightened and my throat became hot. Involuntarily, I began to grind my teeth, but I had to keep my composure.

"Oh, … uh … okay then," she said, stumbling over her words. "Well, we appreciate your cooperation."

"Sure thing, Hillary! I'll see you in a little while." I couldn't help but chuckle after I ended the call. We already had too many people in my department, which negatively impacted our commissions, and now they were doubling the size of the department. It made no real sense for the business, but plenty of sense if the goal was to edge out the workers they couldn't outright eliminate. I had too much pride to give her the satisfaction of getting a rise out of me or sending HR after me, again. I didn't have too much pride to pretend like I had fallen in line.

As hard as I knew it would be to do so, I was thinking more and more about starting my own firm. At least then, I knew I would be under decent leadership. As I walked into the office, my phone buzzed—an email, announcing the hire of the new additions to the sales team.

CHAPTER 9

"I miss you."

"I know this is hard on you, Aiden, and Mitch. Everything comes to pass, right? It will be over soon," I said, partially trying to convince her, partially trying to convince myself.

"When was the last time you slept, and I mean more than a couple of hours?" she asked.

Kaitlyn was worried about me. I wasn't sleeping nearly enough, my blood pressure had skyrocketed to the point of needing medication, and I wasn't interested in interacting with anybody, if it wasn't a necessity. Despite that, we still made time for our date night each week, she made breakfast for me each morning, and I made it a point to text her little jokes throughout the day, just so she would feel that no matter how difficult the situation became, I wasn't letting it get the best of me. I had watched couples go through similar trials and come out in pieces. One of my pals ended up having an affair, which only compounded his problems. Another friend, who was dealing with discord at work, ended up getting a divorce. From what I gathered, he and his wife had been tired of each other for years, and the work stress was the final straw.

But Kaitlyn and I had a rare grit and determination for the survival of our marriage. We both grew up with wonderful examples of how to sustain a marriage. We had seen our parents deal with sickness, unemployment, and several moves, so there were no preconceived notions of simplicity and frolicking into the sunset. We knew marriage would present us with challenges, so we regularly examined our relationship to ensure there were no holes in the life we had built together, nothing that could tear into a gaping crater from which we could never recover.

One year, on her birthday, I had promised her a fancy, dress-up dinner at a new upscale rooftop restaurant. Although Kaitlyn is a stunner in sweatpants—and that's how she feels most comfortable—she enjoys dressing up, but certainly not as much as I enjoy when she is dressed up. I had daydreamed about watching her run her fingers through her short curly hair, trying to nudge that solitary runaway curl away from her shadowed and mascara-dressed green eye, but to no avail. I bought her the perfect maroon cocktail dress, short, with lace on top, and a pair of silver strappy high heels. I couldn't wait to see her this way, unconcerned about her job, unbothered by the weekly stress her friends passed on to her, engaged in conversation with me about politics, what our children might look like someday, and the charming personalities of the African students she fell head over heels in love with when she taught abroad for those years after college.

We both had to get up early the next day for work, so we decided to meet each other at the restaurant for happy hour. My office was only two blocks away, so I anticipated arriving before she would, giving me time to stop and buy that triathlon wetsuit she'd been eyeing for some time.

Since I was never late, I knew Kaitlyn must have been concerned when I didn't show up at the top of happy hour, or the middle, or the bottom, for that matter. I wasn't answering the phone in my office, my cell phone battery had died, and I'd forgotten the charger at home. An unexpected potential client had shown up just minutes before it was time for me to leave. I knew I should have rescheduled with her, but I wasn't sure she would come back. This lady was a high-level prospect, and if I won this account, it would mean the rest of the down payment for our new home. I took the meeting and banked on Kaitlyn's forgiveness.

As the big-name potential client wrapped things up and approached the exit, Kaitlyn appeared behind the elevator doors. Part of me expected fury and possibly tears, but I didn't get any of that. Kaitlyn waved goodbye to the client, kissed my cheek, and placed a blanket from the shop next door onto the floor. In silence, she commenced to spread out a picnic of entrees and red wine from the rooftop restaurant, then patted the blanket for me to join her. Still silent, I did.

Before the apology could avalanche from my mouth, she asked, "Did you close the deal?"

I took a deep breath. "I am not sure yet. She is a real nice lady. Very sharp. I think it went well, especially given the fact she showed up unannounced. I have heard of her doing this to people at other firms before. She likes everyone to be on their toes. Can't say I blame her. She is responsible for the benefits plans for a lot of employees. The advisors she hires need to always be thinking about her company's needs. The surprise appearances are a way to remind them."

She stroked the side of my face. "I knew you must have had a good reason for not coming to the restaurant, so I brought the birthday to you. I hope you like your dish. The waiter said it was a crowd favorite."

"I'm sorry, Kaitlyn."

"What for? This is better."

We enjoyed the office-floor picnic, complete with Kaitlyn in the maroon dress. As she reminisced on failed birthday parties of the past, maneuvering that lonesome curl, I knew that Kaitlyn was far more than I deserved.

I kept waiting for the other shoe to drop, for her to turn into the other, been-married-long-enough Kaitlyn that everyone said would soon emerge, but that never happened. I was one of the lucky ones who got exactly who I signed up for. So when Kaitlyn suggested I take an afternoon to meet with a life coach who could possibly help me game-plan my way out of my present nightmare, I did it. I knew she was coming from a place of loving concern. After all, even Michael Jordan had a coach.

"He's a great guy. My cousin gets advice from him. I think he can help," she mentioned between rolling socks and hanging the nice shirts to air dry in the laundry room. "He recently left a Fortune 500 company where he reported directly to the CEO."

"Wow, so he was big-time. Why did he leave?"

"Because they forced out his boss."

"Seems we already have some things in common." I put a reminder to meet with him in my phone and went to bed.

"How long would you estimate this has been going on again, Ray?" Ricardo seemed more interested than I expected of a man who handles head cases like me all the time.

"Around two-and-a-half years now."

"Okay, tell me how you are. And remember, you can be completely honest. I can't give you the best help, unless you're completely honest."

I was relieved to hear those words. It had been a long time since anyone had my back, like the way Howard, Sean , and Jackson did, before everything fell apart.

Ricardo had set aside two hours for our first meeting. Initially, I didn't think I would need it all, but he was easy to talk to. He asked better questions than, "How does that make you feel?" and about fifteen minutes into our conversation, I felt confident that I would get what I went there for.

I started off by telling him about Howard—how rattling it was to see him unfairly forced out, and how the office environment had quickly grown toxic since his departure. I told him about how they got rid of Jackson, and how Sean, one of the last good guys, had up and left with no warning. I was one of the few seasoned employees who were still standing. He asked me how I was coping with the stress and whether I had confronted the new leadership or not. What he said next confirmed that I had come to the right place for direction.

"Ray, if you're not ready to change firms, what are you ready to do?"
"I'm not completely sure," I responded. "There's really nowhere for me to go. None of our competitors have positions parallel to mine at Fisher. I'm kind of stuck."

"Well, you have a few choices. You could bite down hard, and bow down to Hillary and Ben, which will destroy you in the short and long run."

"Not an option," I replied. "What else you got?"

"If you're up for it, you can orchestrate a massive coup and get all those clowns fired." I must admit, that suggestion made me feel tingly inside, but I wasn't sure I wanted to go that route.

"Or?" I spurred him on.

"Or, since your competitors don't look like they can offer you anything, you could start your own gig," he finished. "Let me ask you something. Do people hire YOU, or do they hire the company?"

"That's easy," I said. "They hire me."

"Well then, buddy, you know your answer."

Ricardo also helped me see that I had become someone I didn't like or recognize, complete with the candy eating and the jaw popping that had emerged from the new habits of walking around all day with clenched jaws and grinding my teeth at night. He also confirmed that I wasn't a lunatic, but a fed-up guy who, because of my career, had become disheartened, confused, and depressed. It was time to come up with a concrete plan to remove myself.

"Ray, I'm pretty familiar with your line of work. I understand how the quick, massive consolidation of the industry has changed things. These large companies think their success is because of their platform, not the people. We both know how twisted and arrogant that thinking is, but it is the reality. Based on what you've told me, it's just a matter of time before they come for your job, and truthfully, you probably won't even see it coming. You are on the menu man. If I were you, I'd be preparing for the worst. I can't tell you what to do, but I can tell you what I'd do." Ricardo had my full attention.

"I'm listening," I said.

"First, save all your files on a flash drive. Do NOT, under any circumstances, save any new files to your computer or the company network. The flash drive is your new best friend. Second, don't tell them the true status of current or prospective clients. If they ask, just be vague. Go full politician on them. If you want to, make up some clients for added sport. Then, let existing engagement contracts expire, and don't make your clients sign any contracts. Work on a handshake or a letter of understanding, instead. Contracts are with the company, not the advisor," he continued. I held my hand up for him to pause while I took notes, then nodded my head when I was ready for him to continue.

"This will help protect you and your family, and that's who you need to be looking out for. To hell with your bosses. You can iron out the details, but this is a good start. But hey, that's just what I would do," he finished, as he shrugged his shoulders.

His proactivity impressed me. His final bit of advice was to write down all the frustrations I had about the job—to write a letter telling the new managers how I felt about them, and then rip up the letter. That sounded like a great idea.

"Remember to rip it up though, Ray," he said.

"I will," I responded.

I didn't waste any time. On the way home, I stopped to buy the flash drive that had the largest memory I could find. As soon as I got home, I furiously began to scratch words on paper with so much zeal that I could barely read my own writing. It turned out to be the best method I had found to remove some of the weight I had been carrying on my shoulders. Before long, I had completed fifteen pages. As I read and reread it, I decided to keep it. The story was too compelling to keep to myself.

CHAPTER 10

The office was filling up again, but with strangers. There were new faces all around, constantly dialing numbers and fast-talking through conversations on the phone. They jotted down notes as they dove straight into personal financial situations of the prospects on the other side of the conversation. I wanted to tell them those things were secondary, but I had long learned that my suggestions were as useful as rotary phones with that crowd. From time to time, I would walk through the office and observe. There wasn't much friendly conversation. There were a lot of closed doors and advisors eating lunch in their offices, alone. I wasn't sure of anyone's name. I kept my head down, focused on servicing my clients better than ever before, and counting the hours until my next gym session.

In a meeting with Hillary, Ben, and their boss, who was simply an older version of Hillary, I was instructed to take only the clients they assigned to me. "We no longer want you cold-calling or finding new business."

They didn't want me going out and finding people who weren't on some list they had compiled. Initially, I did what they ordered, but it didn't take me long to figure out that all referrals through our platform were going straight to the new recruits, and only the new recruits. The only company-generated leads that came my way were the ones no one else wanted. I wasted countless hours every day advising prospective clients that generated absolutely no income for my family, but of course, helped support the corporate platform. It wasn't long before work was costing me money. If I didn't do something, my paychecks would reflect those of the days when I first started at this company, when I was only making enough to pay the rent.

I decided to ignore these orders and do my job, the way that only I could. Since the new employees couldn't stop bragging about the referrals they were getting from Hillary and Ben, I had gotten wind that a large beauty store supplier called Max Express was shopping their 401k administration business and health insurance plan. This account would mean generous reoccurring revenue for the company and a lovely success fee for the salesperson who won the assignment. I knew the Senior VP of Operations of Max Express from Aiden's lacrosse team. I called in a favor, and he was able to get me a meeting the next week. The only schedule I put the meeting on was the one in my personal cell phone.

The morning of the meeting, the CFO of Max Express and I both arrived in the office before anyone else. We quickly discovered that we shared an alma mater, similar tastes in professional football teams, and were involved in veterans' affairs. Thirty minutes of chatter prefaced how I planned to roll out an improved 401K and health insurance plan for their company, which would likely help with employee retention. It turned out he was a friend of Eric's who had heard great things about me from his Senior VP. He had all but decided to work with me, before he even walked into the office.

"So, what would our service agreement look like, Ray?" he asked.

"I'll make it real easy on you. Let's use a month-to-month engagement letter. It's much less legal work, and this way, you can see me in action before signing up for a long-term agreement. If you're not impressed, you can interview other advisors, and there's no red tape to get out of any contracts with me. Sound good?"

He looked at me with a raised eyebrow, then smiled and shook my hand. "I can dig that, friend." We shook hands, and he patted me on the back like an old pal.

The big win I just had reminded me that although the environment was toxic, I hadn't lost the magic touch, and that a well-established reputation was more important than some company's platform. About two weeks later, I checked my bank account for the bi-weekly direct deposit confirmation, but to my surprise, the account didn't reflect the consulting fees that Max Express had paid in advance. I checked again, just to be sure, but found nothing. I called my friend in accounting, and she informed me that Hillary had told her not to pay me.

"You did NOT hear this from me. By the way, I think they are out for you," she whispered. I thanked her graciously for her candor.

With all the coolness I could muster, I walked into Hillary's office. "Where's my money?"

"What money, Ray?" she asked while she applied a fresh coat of lipstick in the new full-length mirror that stood in the corner of her office. Her stoic demeanor made me question if she could be a sociopath.

"You know what I'm talking about. Don't play with me." I had a vision of smashing her mirror into the wall. My anger began to rise, but I caught myself, pressed my top row of teeth onto the bottom row, and maintained my composure.

"Well, sir, if you're referring to the consulting fees from Max Express, which you snatched from the Triad guys, you're not gonna see that money," she answered. Nor will you see any of the fees generated by the 401K and health insurance plans that I heard you were selling them. Seriously, why are you even pitching those plans? They pay the lowest commissions out of all the products we sell. You need to start selling the ones with the highest fees!"

"It's unethical to not pay me, Hillary. On top of that, the plans that I pitch may not pay the company as much in fees, but they are excellent products and are in the best interest of our clients. You will give me my money."

"Well, let's see ….that client wasn't even for you. We'd promised that account to the Triad guys while we recruited them. You didn't document that you'd been communicating with them, but you were. And when you listed that client as yours, they were already listed on someone else's records—you know, the person who was supposed to represent that client in the first place. So if you have a problem, maybe you should check your part in this, General Rogue."

"So what happened to 'putting the best team on the field,' which you and Ben keep jamming into our brains? The Triad team wasn't even remotely qualified to win the Max Express account. I already had a relationship with them; everyone knows that. You should have checked with me, first! The fact that you even tried to steer this opportunity toward them is a violation of our ethics, which you seem not to care about based on your leadership. Excuse me, lack of leadership."

"You're noncompliant and don't understand your place here. So now that our feelings are out in the open, I invite you to leave my office, Ray."

Although I appeared calm on the surface, my heart began to throb. My face was hot. My hands were sweaty. Vengeance was the only thing that could make this right, but I couldn't do it in a way that would make me the villain. I had to flip it. I thought about how my father would have handled it.

My dad was a minister, not one of those fire-and-brimstone preachers, but one whom people actually enjoyed listening to and felt comfortable around in an honest conversation. He was almost as good a minister as he was a father, which is why the community was so drawn to him. The same brand of love and acceptance he extended toward me each day, he extended to his congregation as much as he could. The energy of a room would automatically become more positive when he walked in. Dad made everybody feel important. He didn't become a pastor because of how it would make him look in the community or for prestige of any kind. He just loved God, and he loved helping people. To his humble surprise, he was awarded the position of pastor of a large congregation when he was in his early forties. Even though he knew how much time and effort the job would take, he said yes to the opportunity without hesitation. It was a chance for him to lead other people to live the life of love that he so strived to exemplify.

Twenty or so years into his service, the feel of the surrounding churches began to morph into what resembled rock shows—complete with bands, strobe lights, and fog machines—but Dad didn't want any of that. "If God's not enough to get you to come, then there's nothing I can say to get folks to stay," he would say when approached about changing the way the church operated. He wanted to buck the trend, but a small tribe of three rabble-rousers on the leadership board thought he should have done otherwise.

One evening, when the congregation was supposed to be meeting to discuss the upcoming holiday programs, Dad walked inside to find that the scheduled session wouldn't take place. Instead, there sat two rows full of clergy members and popular young professionals who led Bible studies or hosted events for the church. With Dad sitting in front of the church, the three disgruntled leadership team members, who raised more sand than a herd of stampeding wildebeests, began to rattle off my father's shortcomings one by one, none of which seemed to justify their discontent.

"You didn't stay at the church golf tournament fundraiser the whole time!"

"You were on that mission trip in Honduras when we voted for the color of the new carpet!"

My father, in his way, just sat there and took it, until he had finally had his fill.

"Are you done? Do the frustrations of your life seem any more bearable now?" The audience snickered at Dad's bluntness. It was the trait people seemed to like most about him.

"Look, if this isn't the place for you, if you can no longer enjoy your time here, you are free to leave and find what you need somewhere else. As for the rest of us, we will pray for you to find peace," which he did right there. We never saw the three of them again after that.

So instead of losing my composure over the issue, I followed my father's guidance. "Stay calm, and don't panic." Two days later, I sent an email to the head of human resources, who by then, had seen me more in recent months than all the other years I worked at Fisher, combined. As soon as I typed and sent the message, I saved it in my email folder marked, "Paper Trail." I needed to keep records of every bit of communication. I kept it simple, sweet, and extremely direct.

"Hey Scarlett,

Kind of ironic how the company sent an all-company email stating that it had an upgrade to accounting software, and then a 'crash' of the payment system that prevented employees from getting paid. Even more ironic is that this occurred two weeks before the last two earnings releases. Hope the SEC doesn't start poking around. On an unrelated note, I am owed quite a bit of money, and Hillary and I disagree on when it should be paid. Kindly reach out to her, and let her know that I will be paid in the next week."

I copied Ben and a few of his bureaucratic cronies on the email, just to keep everyone involved honest. I can't imagine what must have gone through their heads. I didn't receive a response to my email, but I was paid in full within twenty-four hours, which was all the response I needed.

CHAPTER 11

The few colleagues who still remained from the better days had heard of my firm stance against Hillary and advised me to lay low for a few days, so I stopped at a café to get some work done. I'd just taken a bite of my ham and cheese croissant and opened my lap top when I heard an unfamiliar voice call my name.

"Hey, hey! Ray!"

I looked behind me, chewing on my croissant, trying to figure out where I might know this lady from. "May I help you?" I asked.

"You don't know me, but I know of you, and I'd like to sit down and speak with you soon, if that's okay." She was bright-eyed and looked excited, feelings I remembered having several years ago, before the office became a snake pit.

"About what?" I asked, hoping I didn't sound like a jerk.

"I'm sorry. How rude am I? I'm Nicole, the Director of Recruiting at Red Rock Consulting. We have had multiple headhunters trying to get you to meet with us ever since Howard left, but you don't call anyone back," she said cheerily.

"Oh, of course! Great company, and your dad, from what I know of him, is the best in the business. Look, I am flattered by the calls, but I don't want you wasting your time. I've built a strong business, so if I were going to make any changes, I'd open my own firm and work for myself. I have to be honest though, your father is the real deal. I'm open to hearing what you have to say." I tried to be the kind of person who didn't pass up an opportunity without gathering all the details, first. If they could offer me a worthy package, and I didn't have to endure the stresses of building a firm of my own, I might be able to be convinced. Every day, that office was sucking the life out of me. I welcomed a smooth transition.

"Well, Ray, I'm glad I bumped into you. I know all about you, how you recently won the Richardson and Max Express accounts. Everybody was pursuing those accounts! Apparently, you can sell a case of Jagermeister to a nun." I smirked, mostly because, unbeknownst to Nicole, my mother-in-law spent three years in a convent. It was hard to keep a straight face.

"Your company's growth has been absolutely amazing," I said. "I see press releases about Red Rock all the time. What you folks are doing is remarkable."

"We sure are, and we want you to be part of it. Look Ray, we are going to respect what you bring to the industry, give you the resources to better serve your clients, and hand you a portfolio of well-established clientele. We have the best corporate culture in the industry with a strong philanthropic component. I understand you started a successful charity, right? We will support your vision. When can we do lunch?" Boy, did

Nicole speak my language. Fisher could have used someone like her to reteach the fundamentals that left with our previous leadership.

"You say when, Nicole," I answered as I tingled with anticipation about work for the first time in several years.

"Tomorrow? Is that too soon?" she asked.

"Not a moment too soon. Here's my mobile number. Call me this afternoon, and we can iron out the details."

"I'll need to talk with our CFO when I get back to the office, but I don't see anything being a problem."

"I understand, but please let them know that I know what I'm worth and not to screw around with the offer. If I am going to make a move, it needs to be a no-brainer," I said.

"Awesome! I can't wait!" she replied, unfazed by my stern response.

And just like that, another piece of my exit plan puzzle seemed to have fallen into place.

The chance meeting with Nicole was a breath of fresh air. She learned how to run a successful business from her father, a trailblazer in our industry. When people left him, it was because they had to move, they were retiring, or won the lottery.

I was hoping my job would be a leadership role, training new hires to be top-tier salespeople, teaching techniques to gain and retain clients, and making sure the team morale was always as high as possible. If so, all it would take for me to commit would be reasonable hours and a solid commission rate.

I took the long way back home. It felt nice to be recruited and appreciated, and I wanted to let the feeling linger as long as possible. The thought of my days being numbered at the beautiful dungeon was enough to make me stroll along with a small hop in my step. Along the way, I noticed a little shop with BBQ supplies in the window. My backyard kitchen was probably covered in cobwebs by now. I hadn't even walked back there in weeks, maybe months. Our backyard used to be abuzz with cookouts and families from the neighborhood every other weekend, but sadly those celebrations were just one of the many things I simply didn't have the energy for, anymore. I had become a recluse, but for the first time in months, I felt like firing up the grill. Kaitlyn's family would be up for it, for sure, and we could invite the kids from Aiden and Mitch's lacrosse teams. It would be nice to bring the yard back to life.

CHAPTER 12

Taking Ricardo's advice, I meticulously planned for my departure. I allowed contracts to expire. I created prospects that didn't really exist, and for extra satisfaction once I was gone, I had already begun constructing my farewell letter. The contract with my new company, which was going to pay almost double what I already made, was signed. Giving two-week's notice wasn't useful, as they would send anybody, no matter how productive or respected, home as soon as they announced they were leaving.

Usually when an employee leaves a company, they get the opportunity to tell everyone goodbye and disperse their new contact information. People who had worked beside me for years were gone, and if we didn't already have their personal mobile number or email, we had no idea when they had actually left, where they were now, or how to get in touch with them. I came to find out this was intentional.

One afternoon in the gym, I ran into a guy I knew from a different department. He had been miserable too, but already escaped for a much better position. We started to run through the list of all the old friends who weren't there anymore from the good old days, and we realized that none of those former coworkers had said goodbye to us.

"Well, it wasn't because they didn't try to say goodbye," he informed me between sets of push-ups.

I raised an eyebrow as he continued.

"It's just the way the email filters are set up." He gulped his water loudly and panted a little.

"What do you mean the way the email filters are set up? What does that have to do with anything?"

"The filters are set up to scan emails and keep certain ones from going out to the email distribution lists. Fisher filters anything that mentions resignation—anything at all that suggests an employee may be leaving. Any word they think might be remotely related to resignation flags the system for review or deletion. It's a pretty sophisticated system."

"These brainwashing control freaks censor our emails for goodbyes? Are you kidding me?"

I had seen the way those two tyrants assassinated the characters of those who escaped before me, and I was determined not to allow that to happen. There was no way I was about to let them lie to the masses, claiming that I couldn't handle the pressure of the job or I needed to take a salaried position because my production was down and I could no longer make ends meet. I had given too much to that company, and recently, I had given up so much because of that company. I couldn't let them cross the finish line of my character before I did. They had said these things about coworkers, my friends, but I had already known these people were leaving, so I knew the stories we were told couldn't have been true.

CHAPTER 13

Paul is my brother-in-law, but I have known him since I was in the sixth grade. He is a technology genius and named inventor of fourteen patents.

"If all you want is an email to go out to everybody, it can be done," he assured me. "Is your IT person located in your office, or are they remote?"

"The office," I said.

"Great! That will make it easier. I wanna introduce you to a friend of mine. He will cut through their precious system like a hot knife through butter. We need to see him as soon as possible though, because he is heading back to Warsaw in about a week or so."

Paul immediately set up a lunch meeting with Artúr, one of his software buddies from college. Artúr held several advanced degrees from one of the most prestigious technology schools in the country, and he was considered an expert in the Eastern European world of technology. If anybody could handle an email system, it was him.

We sat in the back of the swanky new restaurant in town, and Paul sent a text to Artúr to let him know our booth was in the back. Moments later, six feet, six inches, and 250 pounds of man rounded the corner and wrapped Paul in a bear hug. I knew it must have been crushing him; this guy didn't look like he ever missed a workout.

They talked for a minute before he introduced himself to me. His handshake was curiously soft for a man of his stature. He looked scary, but he was laid-back.

We briefly made small talk before jumping into business. Prior to our meeting, Paul had already explained my situation to Artúr, and his team had begun their "discovery" phase. Artúr stated that getting my farewell email out through their firewall and other security measures would not be a problem, although he did give them credit for having such a robust system simply to monitor employee emails. His team had identified several minor flaws with their Internet security, the most glaring being its remote access. Exploited properly, these little holes would bring the company to its knees.

To its knees? I thought. *I just want to get my farewell letter through their email filter.* But Artúr was that way, all or nothing.

He explained to me that his company identifies weak points in large-scale IT infrastructures. His clients are mainly large online retailers, banks, and accounting firms who pay big money to have these corrected before their systems get hacked, resulting in huge data breaches, which leads down a death spiral of lawsuits and trending news stories that all companies would rather avoid.

"You have many IT personnel in your office, am I right about that?" asked Artúr.

"That's right," I replied.

"Can I see your company laptop?" Paul had told me to bring it, along with the charger. I turned it on and logged into the VPN feature, which allows for remote access to the company's server, at which point, Artúr snatched it out of my hands. He paused for a moment, scanned the screen, and began to type faster than I had ever seen before. He never looked down at the keys. My brain took a few moments to catch up with what he was doing.

He asked me some seemingly meaningless questions while he pounded away at the keyboard. Suddenly, the computer squealed. Heads all around the restaurant looked in our direction before it stopped. After that, Artúr plugged a strange contraption into the USB port, a homemade device that was about two inches wide and three inches long. My laptop made the sound again for ten long seconds, then stopped. Artúr smiled, turned off the computer, and handed it back to me.

"What the hell just happened?" I asked.

"Artúr infected your computer with a homemade virus that there is no defense against," Paul said.

"How do you know that, Paul?" I was in limbo, somewhere between being confused and impressed.

"Just trust me," Artúr interjected, "and don't ask too many questions," he warned as he sipped his drink. He winked. I obeyed.

Artúr assured me that the laptop was fine, but to an IT professional, it would seem like it was infected with a virus. I was to call the IT person in my office directly, not the help desk, which was traditional protocol. He then handed me one of the funky contraptions he'd plugged into my computer.

"What do I do with this?" I asked.

"Once you are in the IT person's office, plug this into their computer. Leave it there until the light turns red. You must leave it there until you see the red light; otherwise, it won't work." His stern voice, coupled with his thick Eastern European accent, made the meeting seem that much more official. I agreed to do as I was instructed. I had known the IT guy for ten years, so my visit wouldn't seem out of the ordinary.

"Then what?"

"This is where you stop asking questions," Paul answered.

Artúr smiled, "No, no, it is okay. We are among trusted friends. Here's how it is going to go down. The device you plug into their USB drive has a program that will scrape every bit of data from their hard drive, as well as shared company drives. Since this person is in IT, it will capture the login credentials, email addresses, phone numbers, personnel calendars, and anything else contained in email and calendars."

I had no idea where this was going.

"With this data," he continued to explain, "we will be able to see every person's calendar and know when the IT staff will be as scarce as possible—for example, when they are in other meetings, on vacation or conferences, things like that. This will tell us the optimum time to send your email."

I raised an eyebrow in confusion. Artúr smiled with satisfaction, knowing I had no idea how this was relevant.

"Remember that the device you plant captures the login credentials, titles, and phone numbers for everyone in the company. Once my team decides the staff is at its lowest headcount for the moment, they will take the next step. It involves several thousand electronic robots, better known as just 'bots,' that will hammer your employer's servers worldwide. It will appear that these bots are trying to steal information contained within their human resources system."

"Wait ... so we are going to distract them by trying to steal a bunch of birth dates and home mailing addresses?" The more he explained, the more confused I became.

Artúr continued, "It will appear that these bots are scrambling the personal data of thousands of employees. Birth dates are only the start. Names, direct deposit information, bank accounts, benefits selections, Social Security numbers, 401(k) plans—they will all be completely scrambled, and there is no way to correct them, other than to start over from the very beginning."

"Damn," I said and sat back, amazed.

Artúr smile and chuckled, "Yes, damn."

I explained to Paul and Artúr that all I wanted to do was get my email out so that they couldn't make up lies and say I was fired. This seemed like a massive cyberattack with serious ramifications if we got caught. Artúr assured me that we would not be caught, since all his operations were run out of Belarus. I had heard of Belarus; it is where many of the brightest tech minds live. It is also where many of the world's cyberattacks originate, and I wasn't sure we needed to make this thing so extreme.

Artúr continued, "Another set of bots will automatically put emergency IT requests to their designated corporate contact. Each IT person will receive about five requests every minute, from a legitimate employee's email address, without them even knowing. Those that are on watch will be overrun quickly between the cyberattack and all the emergency tickets. They will be paralyzed. For added insurance of our success, my call center will be calling the same IT professionals, stating they need assistance with their computers and that they fear a virus. The names and phone numbers on the company's caller ID system will all match. Although the calls will be coming from outside the company, no one will be able to tell. The phone systems and email servers will crumble within an hour of the attack.

"Then, your email will be permitted to go to as many people that you wish. They will not be able to stop it, and there will be no one available to turn off your email because they will be too busy fighting off a wide-scale attack." He laughed, adding, "Besides, none of their login credentials will work after that, anyway."

It was an over-the-top, diabolical, well-thought-out plan, and it was genius.

The very next day, I did as instructed. I went into the IT guy's office and stated I had an issue with my computer. He started working on it, and after a few minutes, he said he was on his way to smoke a cigarette and asked if I could come back. While he went down the elevator, I slipped back into his office, as if I belonged. I plugged Artúr's homemade device into my coworker's USB drive. While I waited, I sent a text to Artúr and Paul, stating that I was alone in the IT person's office. Artúr fired back, telling me to let the light turn yellow, if I had the time. A few seconds later, the light turned red. I waited, tense, my eyes scanning from the light to the door over and over for another forty-five seconds before the light turned yellow. I snatched the homemade apparatus and left the office.

Once I was downstairs, I texted the group to let them know the light had turned yellow, and I made a clean getaway. We made plans for dinner that night.

❖

I handed the device to Artúr. With a big smile, he caressed it like one would a baby rabbit, treating it gingerly.

He plugged the thing into his computer, and his eyes grew wide as his fingers danced around the keyboard for no less than thirty minutes. Paul and I sat there, sipping drinks, not knowing what to say. Artúr announced the exact day and time when the IT staff would have nearly 75 percent less staff. That is when the attack was to be unleashed. Ninety minutes later, my resignation letter was to be sent from a remote location.

All that was left to do was to write my farewell letter and wait for Artúr's text that would instruct me to hit "send." His team would take care of everything else. The impending moment of freedom was exactly four days, fifteen hours, twenty-three minutes, and fifty-seven seconds away. I grew giddier by the second, as 12:44 p.m. crept closer and closer…

Hillary would certainly be monitoring my email to try to pick off any assignments I was working on or any new leads that might come in. Instead of her being able to call these people and state that I was fired and someone else would be handling their accounts, they would simply contact me at my new email address. For yet even one more poke in the eye to

Hillary and Ben, Artúr worked his magic and extracted the company's internal email distribution lists. I would be able to use the company's own email distribution lists to send my new contact information from my new company email address, and the "All Management" list would provide the most satisfaction.

When I sat down to pen my resignation, it flowed from me effortlessly.

Dear Friends and Fisher Family:

How do I say thank you? How do I thank a company who gave a young college grad a shot in an industry dominated by seasoned financial advisors? There are so many whom I want to thank for helping me so much over the last 22 years. Without the dedication and hard work of our staff, I would have never had the success that God has blessed my family with. Thank you, to our cutting-edge marketing team, which provided me with the tools to achieve Producer of the Year for the region multiple times. And thank you, to our dedicated research team that helped me provide excellent service to my clients. It is because of our amazing staff's dedication that I was able to have great success and thoroughly enjoy the journey.

When I arrived here at Fisher, several veterans took me under their wing. These people molded me into who I am today. My sincere thank you to our friends Jackson, Sean, and most importantly, our excellent leader Howard, who inspired us and had our backs, every step of the way.

I would like to thank Benedict Bonaparte, Hillary and her boss, and the multiple sales managers brought in over the last three years to help expand our service lines and implement new procedures and policies to ensure that Fisher maintained its market share. I commend all of them for their commitment to their vision.

Your pal Ray is going in a different direction. However, I am here for you anytime I can be of assistance, whether personally or professionally. Please do not hesitate to contact me. I will not be far away. If you want to do lunch-I am buying.

Your friend,
Ray

I sighed more deeply than ever before.

CHAPTER 14

"Hey there, Ben!" I was pregnant with sarcasm.

"You son of a—"

"Whoa there, Ben!" I exclaimed. "Watch that dirty little mouth, friend."

Ben was livid and panting like a wild animal. I put him on speakerphone and listened to his every word as I sat on the other line in my home office, feet propped up on an ottoman, enjoying the kale smoothie I'd made for my midmorning snack. I don't remember a day when I felt more satisfied—the way he should have felt, too—considering the number of four-letter words he dropped during that conversation must have broken some kind of record. He even taught me a few new ones.

"You freaking coward, you couldn't even tell us to our faces! You just…left!" squealed Ben.

"I wasn't about to become a victim of another one of your couldn't-handle-the-pressure lies, or one of the random executions like Jackson, firing him for no reason three weeks before Christmas without an explanation. My resignation, my terms, friend." I slurped the last bit of my smoothie through my straw as loudly as I could. "Heck, you were probably hoping to do the same thing to me if I hadn't just won the Max Express account."

Ben commenced to calling me more names I'd only heard in violent R-rated action movies, and I must say, every moment only served to reassure me that I had made the right decision.

He finally stopped ranting long enough for me to ask if we were done.

"You'll be done when I'm finished with you," he threatened.

"Easy man, it's just business. Just like the conspiracy you and Hillary led to sabotage my career. Sure, you would let me buy you lunch all the time—which, by the way, would have gotten you fired at most Fortune 500 companies—all the while, doing whatever you could to undermine my reputation with clients. I'm out of your hair, so you should be happy, right? You got what you wanted, so congratulations, but now you have to compete against me, and your division's market share just got cut in half."

I was waiting for another barrage of foul language and threats, when instead, all the sudden he calmed down, almost as if a muscle relaxer had kicked in. "So, when is your last day?"

"As of yesterday, you were relieved of your duties as my boss. Your services are no longer needed."

"Where is your laptop?"

"It's at my house. I live in a gated community, and the guard won't let anyone in without written permission. There are several residents in my neighborhood who require high security, so I wouldn't suggest you try to come get it. You don't need my computer anyway, since your IT people can shut my email off in about thirty seconds." I smiled as I thought about the untruth of that statement.

He hesitated before he choked, "We've already done that, but we do need the laptop back." I found his pause and the trembling in his voice rewarding.

"Sure thing, man. I will return it, once the company pays me the rest of the money I have been owed for over three weeks. Then you can have your $600 laptop back. No problemo."

I knew Ben wanted the laptop, not just because it was company property, but for all the files that were on it. Little did they know that I had not saved a file to the hard drive or company server for months, and there would be no helpful files to recover. Flash drives are beautiful little devices. Ben sat silent for a few short seconds, resetting his voice.

"I need to know the status of your former clients and an overview of the services we are providing them, so Hillary can decide who to give your accounts to."

"Sure. Which of my clients do you want to talk about?"

"Let us start with Max Express. They just signed up with us, so there should be another two or three years left on the engagement agreement, right?" His voice was quivering.

"No. I only signed them up to a monthly agreement. It expires tomorrow, and they're coming with me," I answered with pure confidence.

A pleasantly uncomfortable silence ensued.

"Well, what about the Richardson account? How much time is left on that contract?"

"Yeah, about that one. It expired about four months ago, and you won't be hearing from them, anymore." I was laughing on the inside.

"Jasmine Enterprises"

"What?"

"Jasmine Enterprises"

"Sorry Ben, I have no idea what you are talking about," I said, as I racked my brain trying to remember this company.

He snapped back, "Your monthly report has them listed as a prospect that you had multiple meetings with. I need to know where this pursuit stands, so I can give it someone else!"

"Ohh, yeah, I remember now! Yep, that company, plus all the other companies on that page, and flip the page, do you see that list, too?" I asked, hardly able to keep my composure for what I was about to say.

"Yes, are these all prospects?"

"Sure, if you count made-up prospects as prospects," I answered.

"What do you mean made-up prospects?" he asked me.

"Just what I said—I made them all up. They don't exist. They are as fake as the leadership skills that landed you and Hillary the jobs you have, today." Satisfaction bolted through my body.

Now Ben, as you can expect, my phone is insane right now. I gotta run, but if I may, let me offer you a suggestion. Hang a headshot of Howard in that office to remind folks of what a real leader looks like. Have a nice day, Ben."

Shortly after I hung up, I began to get text messages from my company friends telling me whatever I did, not to reply to the email Ben had just sent out. Imagine how double-minded he appeared when I had just sent that email, thanking him for his encouragement, leadership, and service toward the company, and then, minutes later, the entire office received an email from Ben saying that it only made sense for me to leave the company so that I could fully focus on my charity instead of splitting my time between my charity and clients. He called my resignation unprofessional. Hardly anyone found his email credible. It came after my email, and only served to make Ben look vindictive. Had he not sent this email in an attempt to discredit my name, no one would have known that management had been completely blindsided. But his accusations of not paying attention to my clients because of my charity, acting unprofessionally, and stating they had no idea I was considering leaving, after seeing the email I sent first, was the beginning of everyone seeing the truth of management's incompetence. I chuckled at the manifestation of their lack of skill.

CHAPTER 15

"Ben began to do what anyone in his situation would do. He panicked for a while and paced through the office, then disappeared into a conference room. He was on the phone, yelling. It was crazy, but entertaining, I can't lie," Cindy said and she flipped through the café's menu. She had called me to catch up, and I was thrilled that she was willing to share details of what went down in the office the day of my escape.

"What about Hillary?" I asked.

"She stayed in her office, for the most part. A bunch of senior leadership came in and out of the building that day. Some waved at us, some didn't. They were sliding in and out of Hillary's office, really quiet. When the last one left, Hillary stomped through the hall, saying stuff we couldn't understand. She was grumbling and hissing, I thought she might explode. Then Ben burst into your office opening the file drawers and slamming them. Actually, that's when he got on the phone. He didn't know what the heck to do."

We both ordered our lunch, and Cindy kept talking. There was a relaxation in her face that I hadn't seen in years.

"Nobody could login to our work accounts, so I'm assuming they couldn't, either. So we all just sat back in our chairs and watched the storm unfold.

You shoulda been there," she giggled and looked down at the ground. "I shouldn't laugh."

"Why not? Funny is funny, right?" I comforted her.

I could imagine how those phone calls played out. Ben called folks to tell them I wouldn't be handling their accounts, anymore. They had never heard of me, because those leads weren't real. Ben looked even more ridiculous than before. Repeat.

"How long did this go on?" I asked.

"Not that long. We all left for the day after Ben slammed the door to his office so hard that it broke the glass in his window."

"So what's your plan? You gonna stick around?"

"I'm not sure, yet. If they are, I'm not, but they may not be around too much longer. We'll see. I've given so much to the company for so long," she trailed off.

"Be more loyal to yourself than to that company, Cindy. I still wish that things had not gone the way they had, but I didn't have a choice. They were stealing money from my family, I was pinned to the wall, and I went total honey badger on them. So whose fault is it when an employee takes such evasive action, like I did?"

I hoped that Cindy would understand that her job wasn't worth her sanity. I continued my rant. "Is it the employee's fault, or that of the people who oppressed and essentially tormented that person? I blame them for my actions. They deliberately poked this bear multiple times, and then they acted surprised when they got the claws, the jaws, and a load of poop on their hands!" Cindy laughed in agreement.

I wallowed in my sense of accomplishment, as I reflected on how well the plan worked. I had let all the engagement contracts expire, and my clients had gotten my new contact information. I made sure that every trace of my time at Fisher was gone, which included an immediate 50 percent hit to the division's revenue the moment I left. Hillary and Ben would receive no bonuses until they could replace my revenue, which I predicted would take at least three years, assuming they didn't get fired in the interim, which might have happened had I answered the chief compliance officer's phone call about why I left. My guess was that he was still trying to figure out how my email slipped through the company's sophisticated detection system.

CHAPTER 16

Spring was in full effect. I was sitting on the back porch, watching the budding leaves sway in the breeze, when my phone buzzed. It was Paul inviting me to dinner. Artúr was in town, and we could finally talk about how well his plan had worked.

We met at what had become our spot, the same restaurant and table. The energy was much lighter than our last meeting. Artúr's expression reflected of satisfaction, as I filled him in on how flawlessly his plan had been executed. I recounted phone calls and showed him text messages from that day, the day of my escape. They couldn't quite believe that we'd beaten the email system the way we did, and my email had made it out first. Fisher was out of luck, and their luck steadily grew worse as competitors, clients, and leaders from other companies began to call to inquire about what was going on. We howled with laughter as we imagined what it must have been like to see those pompous swindlers come undone at the realization of what had happened.

What I wanted Artúr to know most were the two compliments I received about his part in the ordeal. Two old friends, who received the email, called to say that they loved it, but mostly, they wanted to know how we got through my employer's email filters. It turned out that both of them were in horrific work situations as well, and they wanted to leave in the same fashion as I did. When Artúr learned that I wanted to forward his contact information on to them, he slid back in his seat and smiled.

The silence finally broke when Artúr reached into his leather backpack and retrieved two small, brown paper lunch bags. He placed one in front of Paul, and one in front of me. Paul quickly snatched his and tossed it into his man-purse. I sat in confusion.

"It's your taste of the action, friend," Artúr answered before I had a chance to ask. Inside the sack were stacks of crisp hundred-dollar bills. "There's $100,000 in that bag, so don't lose it," he whispered as he chuckled to himself. "Go buy a boat. Take your sons and father fishing as much as possible."

I sat in disbelief of the amount of money sitting in front of me. I'd told Kaitlyn that someday we would have a boat and take the family fishing, the way Howard used to take me out on his boat. He explained that Fisher hired his company to fix the holes in their technology systems. The money I now held was a referral fee. That was when it hit me. The month before, Fisher's stock plummeted eight percent in one trading session when they had missed earnings. In their earnings release, Fisher's CFO cited a "highly necessary, costly and unpredictable IT expense." Many of Fisher's clients had read much deeper into the CFO's statement and assumed that Fisher had been hacked, exposing their confidential data and that of their employees. The alleged breach was all over the business news channels, and panic spread to investors, triggering a huge sell-off, and crushing the stock's value. Paying Artúr's team to correct the weaknesses in Fisher's technology infrastructure was well worth their investment.

But as much as I wanted to take the money, I just couldn't. I slid the bag back across the table.

"You'll probably think I'm a chicken, but if I take this money, I'll sleep worse than I did before I left Fisher. I'm sorry, man."

Paul asked, very slowly, "Are you suuuuuuuure, Ray?" He grabbed my hand as the bag sat halfway across the table.

"Yeah, I'm sure." Paul shrugged his shoulders, patted his man-purse that safely held his brown paper bag, and winked at Artur.

We sat around for a while, re-enacting the panic that must have overcome the office, that day. Artúr later revealed that what had been the most difficult part of my escape plan was now simple. He'd acquired a little device that could swipe all the necessary information off a company's computers, remotely. Instead of trying to plug devices into the IT person's computers like I had to, they could now do it from the parking lot. Artúr began to explain the technology behind his new toy, but he could quickly tell I had no clue what he was talking about. I recall him saying something about cloning IP addresses and then he lost me. It was over my head.

I texted my two friends to let them know the right people were in town to help them fire their bosses the way that I did, but they had to meet with them within the next day or two.

"These guys are clean-cut. I'm not sure they are that serious about replicating my stunt," I said.

"Well, so were you, until you were pushed far enough," Paul reminded me.

He was right. I had gone from a happy team player who bled the colors of the company to a disgruntled employee of biblical proportions. Artúr and his team used disgruntled employees to open doors for them to extort millions from their employers. Once guys sent out the emails beyond the firewalls and the companies realize they have holes in their systems, they hire Artúr and the crew, for millions, to fix them. I guessed some might say they were in the wrong, but truthfully, they helped me save my career and my sanity. In my opinion, they were the good guys. I invited Artúr and Paul over for dinner before they left town. They could help me break in the new addition to my backyard kitchen, a gorgeous new stainless steel smoker that was the size of a refrigerator.

As I set out the drinks and paper plates for the cookout, Artúr commented, "We passed by your sons' school on the way over. I see they're breaking ground on the east side of the building."

"Yeah, apparently, somebody made a $100,000 anonymous donation for an expansion for their kids. The new computer lab is insane!" Kaitlyn exclaimed.

We all smiled, as we got in line to load up our paper plates.

Epilogue

They say God works in mysterious ways. When it comes to the way things unfolded relating to my career, this adage is an understatement. Watching Howard, our former boss, mentor, and friend deal with his push into retirement infuriated most of our region. Additionally, the leadership who took his place were unethical, and my early attempts to protect my colleagues from their behavior landed me on their naughty list. Apparently, confidential discussions with human resources weren't so confidential. Their plan of revenge was to hire my competitors from another firm, steer all of what should have been my business to them, and tie my hands on pursuing new accounts, so that my career would implode.

If none of this had ever happened, Howard, Sean, myself, and many others would still be working together, dominating the field and maintaining the bottom line for the division at twice what it is today. Instead, we are all at competing firms, and while the trudge toward exiting the company was gut-wrenching, we all came out on top.

Howard now leads a successful firm in a beautiful part of the state. His income is higher than it was before, he works on his photography, and he travels as much as he wants. Four of the largest clients in Fisher's region happily transitioned their business to my new employer, each of which I was told not to pursue. I always wanted to help others build their careers, and now I lead a team of ten producers who are excited to follow my guidance. It is rewarding to see them evolve, both professionally and personally. Lou Holtz's book, *Wins, Losses, and Lessons,* states that being "significant" means that one makes a lasting impression and helps build others' careers. That is the kind of person I aspire to be.

I have competed against, Hillary, Benedict and his "ordained team" five times since I left, and I have won every time. Fisher has gone from the clear leader in the market to being tied with the number three company, which is mine. But I guarantee, we won't be there for long. We continue to gain market share via organic growth, acquisitions of complimentary organizations and a stream of unhappy employees fleeing from Fisher with hopes of joining us.

I must be honest and say that I miss the friends I had made over those 22 years, but we all meet for lunch regularly, and Howard often joins us. We still mesh, as if nothing ever happened, and I pick up our lunch tabs from my expense account, a perk I never had before. I am more than happy to do it.

When Howard left, an entire disheartening culture shift took place that nearly drove me to a nervous breakdown. He would constantly say, "It's all about the people," a phrase that I didn't fully appreciate until the day when all "the people" were gone. It was as if a ton of bricks had fallen onto my groin. I spent 19 inspiring years under unmatched leadership, and three years under the complete opposite. I learned from both, and in my undying quest to find a silver lining in all situations, I have convinced myself that those three years of mental anguish pushed me to somehow become a better leader for others.

It has been almost a year that I pulled off what I consider to be the most epic resignation of all time. The company did not see it coming. Although I had removed the files from my drawers, the top of my desk was completely untouched. My managers believed that they had beaten the spirit out of me, they were completely in control of my future, and that I was close to bowing down to their reign of terror. On the surface, everything looked normal. I even turned in my 30-page business plan for the next year, complete with fake clients, potential clients, and an erroneous marketing plan, complete with financial projections. All of my engagement contracts had expired, ensuring that I could take my clients with me, as they were not bound to stay with my employer. If I hadn't done this, my clients would have been contractually obligated and could not have moved their business to my new company. I had not saved one file to the company's computer or server in many months. With the help of my brother-in-law, Paul, and Artúr's team, we executed what was probably the most sophisticated email heist in corporate America. It was truly a work of art.

Looking back, there is no doubt that I was mentally unstable and failing miserably as a father and as a husband. The years of high stress, anger over how my colleagues were being treated and fear of not being able to provide for my family combined to push me to the edge, hence the scorched earth, total war and take no prisoners policy I implemented. I did what I needed to do to protect my family. My exit did promptly get the attention of Fisher's top brass, which caused them to react.

Today, Fisher employees are no longer able to save a file to anything but the company servers or hard drive. All features that enable a person to save a file to an external device or cloud based offering were intentionally disabled. It was also mandated that everyone share electronic calendars with their superiors and provide explicit details of each and every one of their meetings. They even set up regional teams to enforce these unprecedented micromanagement policies and had surprise compliance inspections on company electronics. Lastly, all sales staff were forced to sign a new 35-page obnoxious employment agreement which included a rigid non-compete clause and a $19,000 annual pay cut for producers that had been with the company for at least four years. Jamming these mandates down producers' throats resulted in another round of defections.

I can't help but still scratch my head as to what I did to deserve such hostility from Hillary, her boss, and Benedict. For Hillary and her boss, it was easy. They are simply mean people with a big empty hole in their hearts. The pleasure they get out of life comes from making others miserable. Ben ... well, he was just following orders so that he could keep his job. It turns out that he applied for many other positions in our industry, but to no avail. His position at Fisher was his only way into the industry, and he had kids in college, so when he sat across from me at lunch, which he often did, and allowed me to pick up the tab, which he also often did, he was conspiring how to destroy my career to please Hillary and her boss. They convinced him that edging me out was best for the company and their bonuses. But how people can be so cavalier about the well-being of others will forever remain a mystery to me.

Several months ago, stock analysts took notice of my former region's stunning $45 million drop in revenue from the prior year. This infuriated several powerful shareholder activists, and they demanded an investigation. The investigation uncovered that nearly every dollar lost was directly related to unhappy producers leaving the company for a competitor and bringing their clients with them. Even more problematic for Fisher, those were reoccurring losses for the indefinite future, which could easily reach $160 million in unexpected losses in under four years.

Hillary and her boss were immediately demoted in a very public manner, although they weren't terminated. Ben was denied the promotion that he had been expecting. He was also placed on probation, forced to take leadership classes, and received a nominal pay cut, but he could ultimately resurrect his career, should he improve his leadership and stay out of trouble. I expect his punishment was lighter, since the investigation determined he was simply Hillary's puppet. He was doing what he felt he needed to do to provide for his family, even at the grave expense of so many others.

I essentially lost three very precious years with my family that I will never get back. However, I have chosen to forgive those who deliberately tormented me—not for their sake, but for my own. I thank God that I am nothing like them, and I pray that I can ensure my boys do not end up in a situation like mine.

At the strong encouragement of my amazing wife, I continued to seek coaching from Ricardo and started seeing a holistic doctor named Ha. My wife wanted me to get off my stress medications, as she was convinced that they had been negatively impacting my personality and decisions since everything went south.

Ricardo continued to deliver sound advice on both life and business. After about ten hour-long sessions, Ha helped me make sense of the last several years. Her explanation was something to the effect of, "You are a caring person, you will do anything to protect your family, and you thrive from comradery. You are also passive aggressive, a trained military professional, and have Post Traumatic Stress Disorder. Your managers tried to destroy the lives of those you cared about. Then, they came after you in full force and were sabotaging your ability to provide for your wife and sons, which you considered—and rightfully so—a deliberate attack on your family. The combination of stress, anger and fear triggered a degree of your PTSD to resurface and sent you to a very troubled place. I agree with your wife that your medications also had something to do with it, and I am very glad we have finally titrated you off them." Her insight was affirming.

Ha further explained that although I had convinced myself I had forgiven my oppressors, I was still extremely angry. I needed to neutralize my rage for my own health reasons. She suggested that I begin by writing a letter to them, whole-heartily telling them off and holding nothing back. When I informed her that Ricardo had given me the same advice over a year prior, and I had already started the exercise, she told me to start over and be sure to rip it up. I agreed, and over the next six months, I would spend at least one hour nearly every night putting my nightmare onto paper. I hope you have enjoyed reading my story. Writing it has helped me forgive them and myself.

Over the past year, more people than I can count on two hands have approached me, revealing disheartening comments and stories that Hillary, her boss, and Ben shared about me while I was still there. Most of them were appallingly false. However, I did find peace in the fact that the attempted slow death of my career was not a figment of my imagination. In fact, it was even more deliberately calculated and mean-spirited than I had ever imagined. God works in mysterious ways, indeed. Turns out that next to marrying my wife, *going in a different direction* was the best decision I ever made.

www.ingramcontent.com/pod-product-compliance
Lightning Source LLC
Chambersburg PA
CBHW070254230526
45470CB00002B/594